The Medical Research Novel in English and German, 1900-1950

The Medical Research Novel in English and German, 1900-1950

Phillip A. Scott

Bowling Green State University Popular Press
Bowling Green, Ohio 43403

To my parents, my wife, and my two daughters,
I lovingly dedicate this book,
a job that I did to the very best of my ability
and saw through to the very end.

Acknowledgments

To the following special persons I give my special thanks:

to Professors Bruno Hannemann, Hugh Witemeyer,
and Robert Fleming of the University of New Mexico
for their guidance and patience;

to my friend Brian Flora
for computer and printer support;

to all the members of my extended family
for their moral support and help with my *other*
responsibilities;

and most of all, to the Creator
for life, intelligence, curiosity, creativity,
and the subject matter for all research.

Contents

Introduction

The portrayal of the doctor in literature is certainly nothing new to the twentieth century, and the phenomenon of the doctor as a writer goes back at least as far as St. Luke of the New Testament. Concerning the physician and belles-lettres, what is unique to this century is the great proliferation of studies of the doctor as a character and as an author. Throughout this century, dissertations, journal and monograph contributions, and bibliographies concerned with doctors in or behind literary works have been published. Recent scholarly studies such as *Medicine and Literature* (1980), the revised edition of *Literature and Medicine: An Annotated Bibliography* (1982), *Disease and the Novel, 1880-1960* (1985), and *The Body and the Text: Comparative Essays in Literature and Medicine* (1990) are evidence of the increasing awareness of and the great interest in the common concerns of the two fields.[1]

It has also been just in the present century that the doctor has been commonly featured as the main character in works of literature. The 1900s have seen the rise of a subgenre referred to here as the "doctor novel" (any novel whose protagonist is at some time a physician or a medical student). There were relatively few doctor novels published before 1900, but so many have been published since then that it is almost impossible to get an exact count.[2]

The sheer quantity of doctor novels is not the only thing which recommends them, however. Though the vast majority of them could be classed with popular romances, some have been written by authors taken seriously by literary critics. William Faulkner's *The Wild Palms*, F. Scott Fitzgerald's *Tender Is the Night*, W. Somerset Maugham's *Of Human Bondage*, and of course Boris Pasternak's *Doctor Zhivago* are all doctor novels by the definition above, and they by no means exhaust the list of the "serious" ones.

The doctor novel is, then, by virtue of its popularity and its contribution to literature, justifiably studied as a subgenre. And the doctor as protagonist is certainly a worthy subject of literary character study: historically, the physician's significance in the average person's life has increased steadily as the practice of medicine has become more scientific. Indeed, many people nowadays are quite dependent on one or more physicians. The comparative study of literary treatments of the doctor therefore has relevance beyond the artistic and academic realm. Just as

1

scholars can find rewards in determining the effects of different portrayals of physicians on the shape, texture, and content of the doctor novel, so the laity can find great value in studying the dramatizations of the medical profession's effects on its practitioners and their families, friends, and patients.

The increasing importance of one particular type of physician, the medical researcher, has given rise to an interesting subtype of the doctor novel. In this study, this subtype will be referred to as the "medical research novel," defined as any doctor novel in which the drive of the protagonist to engage in medical research is an essential part of his or her character, and in which actual conduct of medical research has a major role in the plot.[3] The medical researcher has been responsible for the vast increase in the stores of information helpful and necessary in modern-day medical practice and for the progressive refinement of the techniques of obtaining such scientific knowledge. The general public's interest in medical research has grown in proportion to its awareness of the ever farther-reaching effects of this activity. Increasing awareness of the relationship between health and the environment and of the functioning of body, mind, and spirit as a unit makes the topic of medical research all the more relevant as time goes on.

The portrayal of the modern physician with a scientific curiosity that leads him or her to active medical investigation affords literature a specialized character study. As if medical practice did not offer enough challenges on the professional and private fronts, the doctor-researcher has taken on even more challenges and must meet additional demands. Beyond the normal professional goals of the physician, the researcher has a quest; and it often becomes a cruel, relentless taskmaster, even more inconsiderate of the doctor's personal life than the constant imperative to heal and to save lives. It often drains the researcher's mental and physical—not to mention financial—resources. Because of the goals and demands of research, the protagonist of the medical research novel can exemplify humanity at its best and its worst. And whereas the repercussions of the medical practitioner's actions or inaction might be felt by an individual, a family, or even a community, the repercussions of the medical researcher's activities could be felt by the whole world. Thus, the medical scientist holds in his or her hands great potential, which can be used responsibly, even nobly, or otherwise.

However, the importance of the subject matter of medical research novels is not their only merit. Many of them have considerable literary worth. There is perhaps no finer example than Sinclair Lewis' *Arrowsmith*, first published as a novel in 1925 and awarded the Pulitzer Prize in 1926 (although Lewis refused it). *Arrowsmith* established medical research as a legitimate quest of the protagonist in serious and respectable literature. There were earlier, less successful novels representative of the subtype and many later examples which attained varying degrees of popular and artistic success. Some of them deserve wider recognition and higher praise than they have heretofore received.

For the reasons mentioned, the medical research novel well merits the examination that follows. Since this type of novel is, with very few exceptions, a product of the twentieth century, and since its representatives in world literature are so numerous, this study will deal with only those medical research novels originally published in English or German from 1900 to 1950.[4] Even within these limits, not all of the novels so categorized could be discussed thoroughly in a study of this length; therefore, only seven will be examined in depth. However, references will be made to eleven others by way of comparisons and contrasts.

Although the novels within the scope of this genre study have great similarities in subject matter and plot structure, each is unique, just like each medical researcher in real life. It would be very difficult, therefore, to select the "most typical" medical research novels for examination. A much easier and more meaningful way of characterizing the subgenre will be used. The novels as a body show how the medical research career can affect the doctor's 1) attitudes toward medicine and science; 2) self-image and attitudes toward life and success; 3) physical and mental health; 4) close relationships with other people; 5) attitudes toward social issues, culture, and recreation; and 6) beliefs about the ultimate authority.[5] Therefore, for each category of effect, one or two especially suitable novels will be analyzed in some detail, and others will be discussed as appropriate. Since this is a study in comparative literature, there will be an attempt to discover meaningful differences between the novels written in English and those written in German. Any such differences which come to light will be mentioned in the appropriate categories. The above categories are not, of course, totally exclusive, but they do serve to bring into focus particular hazards and rewards of the medical research career. The principal novels chosen to represent these categories are, respectively, 1) *Arrowsmith* by Sinclair Lewis (1925), 2) *Angela Koldewey* by Betina Ewerbeck (1939), 3) *Viele sind berufen* by Hermann Hoster (1933), 4) *Die Spur* by W.B. Erlin (1947) and *Medical Meeting* by Mildred Walker (1949), 5) *The Fire and the Wood* by R.C. Hutchinson (1940), and 6) *Georg Letham, Arzt und Mörder* by Ernst Weiss (1931).

Although realism and social relevance are great strengths of nearly every medical research novel, one must be cautious about overestimating these novels' documentary validity. The reader of this book should keep in mind that the works discussed, while offering valuable character studies with broad implications, do not necessarily depict the usual experience of typical real-life medical researchers. The authors have created exemplary doctor-scientists who make exceptional discoveries.

Chapter One
Attitudes Toward Medicine and Science

It is not difficult to see why the eighteen authors in the scope of this study (as well as many other authors) each chose to write a novel about a medical researcher. The individual who becomes a physician and goes on to achieve a difficult goal in medical research is especially gifted and diligent. The medical scientist is a person of action who also proves the power of the idea. Just as importantly for the authors, this type of protagonist is, as will be seen, a person of special conflicts. And conflicts are the stuff of literature.

The complications and contradictions in the professional life of the fictional medical researcher provide an excellent starting point for the present study. For this reason, this first chapter is an observation of how involvement with medical research affects the protagonists' thoughts about the ideals and realities of medicine and science. These attitudes are, of course, revealed primarily through the thoughts, words, and actions of the chief characters themselves; but the narrators' and other characters' remarks will also be cited when appropriate.

It is important to note what the central characters consider the most desirable qualities in the doctor and the researcher, and in some cases, it is necessary to observe the main character's deviations from the narrator's standards for the medical researcher. This chapter is thus, in large part, a summation of the subgenre's statements about the necessary and admirable traits of the physician and of the scientist.

The medical researchers' general attitudes toward their dual occupation are just as one might guess. As doctors who become involved in serious medical research, they obviously think that there is significant value in using the scientific method to answer medical questions. They believe that the practice of medicine should involve something other than memorized information, uninspiring routine, predetermined chances of success, and unabashed exercises in business tactics and public relations. These doctors turn to research because they see science as an intriguing positive force with great potential. Most of the central characters develop such a love and respect for medical research that they want to dedicate their lives to it, even at great personal cost.[1]

4

Some aspects of the protagonists' relationships to medicine and science are perhaps less predictable. Research is so attractive to many of the doctor-scientists that they are lured away from medical practice altogether. And for many who try to serve both medicine and science, there are dilemmas.

The basic question for any of the chief characters is which part of the union of science and medicine should receive the emphasis. As it turns out, some researchers are interested in only specific medical applications of scientific discoveries, others see the scientific pursuit of knowledge as an end in itself, and still others fall somewhere in between the two extremes. These distinctions are not merely academic; they have ethical applications as well.

The novel which reveals the most about the protagonist's and others' attitudes toward medicine and science is *Arrowsmith* by Sinclair Lewis.[2] The discussion of *Arrowsmith* will introduce most of the topics to be considered in this chapter, and an examination of other novels' presentations of these and certain other topics will follow. In both sections, statements about the most desirable qualities of the doctor will be dealt with first. A review of the doctor's attractions to medical research will follow. Then there will be a study of conflicts between science and medicine and a discussion of the traits of the true scientist. A look at statements about the limits of medical science will conclude each section.

Martin Arrowsmith, whose career goes through several phases before he dedicates himself entirely to science, has many changes of heart about his professional standards and goals. Preoccupied first with making a living and then with becoming a success, he often loses his idealism. In his biggest personal crisis, during his most important research assignment, he betrays his scientific principles. He cannot abandon them for long, however, because they are so much a part of him. By the end of the novel, he has become the embodiment of those scientific principles and is perhaps an even greater researcher than his mentor.

Originally drawn to the study of medicine by "the lure to questioning and adventure" (7), Martin is dismayed by the largely unscientific instruction at his medical school. Although medicine at this time (circa 1906) has so very much to learn about disease and the workings of the human body, this medical faculty seems little interested in active investigation. Only one professor, Max Gottlieb, appreciates the value and knows the technique of scientific research. The other professors attach much importance to rules of thumb and traditional medical wisdom. To Martin's great displeasure, he is required to memorize dull lists of anatomical terms and treatments whose effectiveness the medical profession has never seriously questioned. The experiments mentioned in his classes are "fussy little experiments, standard experiments, maiden-aunt experiments" rather than what Martin would like to see, "something dealing with the foundations of life and death, with the nature of bacterial infection, with the chemistry of bodily reactions" (22). Unlike the faculty as a whole and all the other medical students, Martin questions whatever has not been proven and thereby, he becomes an annoyance to instructors and classmates alike. Martin complains that his fraternity brothers are, just like their instructors, "the kind that keep medicine nothing but guess-work diagnosis" (32).

After he earns his M.D. degree, however, Martin relies none too heavily on science in his own medical practice. Agreeing with the dean of his medical school that there is too much specialization in medicine, and also concerning himself with basic practical matters, Martin decides to become a general practitioner in his wife's small hometown. He then has to quell his "scientific lust" and desist from "trifling with the drug of research" (117) in order to keep his mind on things like the day-to-day business of developing a practice and becoming accepted in a small town. Since his patients' treatments generally require no advanced scientific knowledge on his part, and since the small-town atmosphere is repressive and antiscientific, Martin becomes mentally lazy and loses touch with new developments in medicine.

Another of Martin's unattainable ideals for medical practice is that it should be divorced from the profit motive. In medical school, Martin is appalled by most of his classmates' attitudes toward studying and practicing medicine. Martin complains that doctoring is just a business to them:

...they aren't trying to learn science; they're simply learning a trade. They just want to get the knowledge that'll enable them to cash in. They don't talk about saving lives but about "losing cases"—losing dollars! And they wouldn't even mind losing cases if it was a sensational operation that'd advertise 'em! (27)

While these students concede that "science is all right in its way" (27), they are really interested in the study of how the doctor can obtain the best office location and best social contacts. One of Martin's fraternity brothers expresses the essence of this commercial mentality when he says that Martin's scientific idol, Prof. Max Gottlieb, "might have been a first-rate surgeon, and made fifty thousand dollars a year" (37).

Throughout his career, Martin encounters this mentality often enough and sometimes in himself. With a wife to support, he frequently has to consider the financial side of things. On the other hand, after a year and a half in his own practice, he wants to change the system wherein every doctor is primarily a businessman competing with other doctors. Later, as assistant to the director of public health in a midwestern city, Martin is disgusted by "the slimy trail of the dollar" in even the "most ardent eloquence" of his superior (218). But then as a pathologist in a prestigious, blatantly commercial clinic in Chicago, Martin succumbs to the aura of the place. He who once thought most surgeons "merely good carpenters" (111) is awed by the distinguished, perfectly dressed, highly skilled specialists who perform many more operations than are medically warranted. He is also awed by the salary he is offered to do routine laboratory work. His is "the respect of the poor and uncertain for the rich and shrewd" (259).

Martin, who has admired the attitude that healing is an end in itself and that the doctor should be content to serve humanity, can never fully adopt this frame of mind for his own. As an intern, though theoretically motivated by the idea of "the physician's immediate service to mankind" (112), he becomes more driven by the feeling of power and the "incessant adventure" of ambulance work (115). The respect shown him at accident scenes is "endlessly stimulating to his pride" (115). By comparison, his hospital rounds are dull. He sympathizes with the suffering of the patients, but after seeing their pain day after day and dressing the same wounds again and again, he wants to go on to new experiences (115).

Some people would suggest that attending to just the physical needs of patients is unsatisfying because it is only part of the doctor's job, but Martin never subscribes to this idea. When a fraternity brother, a minister wanting to become a missionary physician, says, ". . . the glory of being a doctor is that you can teach folks high ideals while you soothe their tortured bodies," Martin suggests that peoples' ideals should be let alone (18). He maintains this position throughout the novel.

Martin's dissatisfaction with general practice comes not because he cannot reach his patients' spirits but because he does not feel challenged or inspired. To give himself more of a challenge and a greater sense of effectiveness (not to mention the feeling of power and respect), Martin takes on the duties of county health superintendent. He is, as the dean of the medical school observes earlier in the novel, "a passionate fellow, not a drudge" (117-18).

Martin's sudden interest in public health is largely due to a new passion he has found in the war on disease being waged by independently wealthy and internationally known Gustaf Sondelius. In a stirring lecture, the great "soldier of science" asserts that the world must literally mobilize against disease and that "public health authorities must supersede generals and oil kings" (164-65). Under the influence of Sondelius' thinking, Martin feels that the best doctors, for whose profession a healthy population would be "the worst thing in the world," must be made autocratic public health officials (165). The ironic narrator adds that people must then somehow be persuaded to obey these new officials and to stop being sick so often. Martin says of Sondelius' work, "That's what I want to do! Not just tinker at a lot of worn-out bodies but make a new world!" (175).

Like many visionaries, Martin begins to feel that he should have unlimited authority to carry out his mission. He announces to his wife Leora that with the aid of a Sondelius, he would make people and their domesticated animals healthy "whether they wanted to be or not" (173). Before he has even assumed his first duties as a public health official, he informs some farmers that they have no right to have so much tuberculosis and tells them that they should burn down their houses (165). During the course of his three public health jobs, Martin feels justified in employing heavy-handed measures such as tearing down and burning some flimsy, disease-infested tenements, having forcibly relocated the tenants.

No zeal or enjoyment of power, however, is enough to keep Martin in the service of public health. The bad example of his superior Almus Pickerbaugh, "the two-fisted fighting poet doc" (242), shows Martin that not every method is worthy just because the goal is. The "holy frenzy and bogus statistics" (216) of this self-styled scientist, who is nothing more than a master of public relations and hoopla, grate against Martin's respect for truth. Furthermore, by the time strong resistance from people in high places forces Martin to get out of public health work, he has had enough of "all these humanitarians that are so busy hollering about loving the dear people that they let the people die" (231).

Martin is never long without a passion, however—without a specific cause in which to believe and a hero to emulate. As one enthusiasm cools, another is getting ready to burst into flame. A new "god" always arises to slay the one he has last revered (178). Martin's first and last passion in adulthood is scientific research, whose principles are embodied by Max Gottlieb, an unappreciated genius who once worked with "Father Koch" and "Father Pasteur." This passion, unlike the others, never dies although for relatively brief periods of time it is replaced or suppressed. Martin's role model in general practice, "the highest calling in the world" (118), is "Dad" Silva, the dean of the medical school. And Martin's zeal for public health is, as mentioned, largely due to his fascination with Gustaf Sondelius. Of course, these three passions represent not only career phases but also important differences in priorities. Each shift in allegiance is the culmination of an inner conflict which upsets Martin's equilibrium for a time.

The great ongoing conflict in the novel is between medicine and science. Early in his career as a medical student, Martin falls in love with "the hard sureness of science" (28). In his junior year, he confesses, "I'm not much of a medic. I like the lab side....And I don't think much of the bedside manner" (56). As an ardent disciple of Gottlieb, he believes that the truly noble goal is to discover "the Why, the underneath principle" (53). Martin's first original research feels like "his first lyric, his first ascent of unexplored mountains" (53). However, when he has to think very practically about choosing a career, he is swayed by Dean Silva's praise of the country doctor, "priest and father of his people, sane under open skies, serene in self-conquest" (112). Martin is by this time, because of a falling-out with his mentor, "partly freed from the tyrannical honesty of Gottliebism" (109). He feels that medical practice will be a warm, humane refuge from the coldness and hardness of science: "It warmed him to escape from Gottlieb's ice-box into Dean Silva's neighborly world" (109). It is hard to fault the dean's praise of "the men who took the discoveries of Gottlieb's gods and turned them to the use of human beings—made them come alive" (117). Nevertheless, Martin's absence from the laboratory makes him homesick for "the thrill of uncharted discoveries, the quest below the surface and beyond the moment, the search for fundamental laws which the scientist...exalts above temporary healing" (116). Therefore, when Martin decides that he will become an "Artist Healer" as Silva wants (117), he is attempting a compromise: "If he ached a little for research and Gottlieb's divine curiosity—well, he would be such a country doctor as Robert Koch!... He would have a small laboratory of his own" (112-13).

Intermittently throughout the middle section of the novel, Martin conducts research on his own. His scientific work is always more meaningful to him than what he does for a living, but he keeps his private curiosity in check by reminding himself of the importance of his current paying job and the after-hours activities which promote it. At one point, he tries to convince himself that the desire for scientific precision is simply his hobby (217); but after he has had enough of public relations and pseudo-science, he is "wild to get back to research" in a serious way (230). During this middle period of his career, he even manages to publish the results of his private project.

On the basis of his research paper and with the influence of Max Gottlieb, Martin is hired as a full-time research scientist at the McGurk Institute of Biology, where Gottlieb now works. As a member of the Institute, Martin feels that he is part of a "godly association" and has "come home" to his teacher and to proper work (265-66).

The most dramatic battle in the conflict between science and medicine must still be fought after Martin has already started to make a name for himself at the Institute. In this battle, Martin's allegiance to science requires him to violate his oath as a doctor. Sent to test his newly developed plague vaccine in the epidemic raging on the Caribbean island of St. Hubert, he is to inoculate only one part of the population and keep careful notes on the selection procedure and the results. Gottlieb, now the director of the Institute, has warned Martin that it will not be easy to withhold the vaccine from roughly half of the people as he must if the experiment is to prove anything. In order to benefit future generations, Martin must refuse to indulge in pity for people who are dying now. Like Gottlieb, he disdains "the doctors that want to snatch our science before it is tested and rush around hoping they heal people, and spoiling all the clues with their footsteps" (267). Understanding what his situation will be, Martin promises to "harden his heart and keep clear his eyes" (333) although Gustaf Sondelius, his partner on the expedition, wants to vaccinate everyone on the island. Even within the specially commissioned group, there is a conflict between the interests of medicine and those of science.

On the island, Martin at first stands firmly by his scientific principles though he does waver when he sees and hears and smells the horrors of death all around him. He is tempted to "give up the possible saving of millions for the immediate saving of thousands" (358), and it occurs to him that Gottlieb, "in his secluded innocence" (359), has not appreciated the difficulty of the experimenter's situation here. But still Martin swears that he will not "yield to a compassion which in the end would make all compassion futile" (359). He tells the special board hearing his request for permission to conduct the experiment that "mankind has ever given up eventual greatness because some crisis, some war or election or loyalty to a Messiah which at the moment seemed weighty, has choked the patient search for truth" (361). After obtaining permission to experiment, he withstands great public pressure to give the vaccine to everyone. He boasts, even after Sondelius dies of the plague, "I'm not a sentimentalist; I'm a scientist!" (365).

However, when Martin loses his wife Leora to the epidemic, he breaks under the emotional strain. He damns experimentation and vaccinates indiscriminately. When a colleague tries to hold him to proper experimental procedure, Martin snarls, "What do I care for your science?" (376). Despite his later attempt to salvage a part of the experiment when he has recovered somewhat from his grief, Martin cannot regain the forfeited chance to procure meaningful, reliable data.

Having betrayed his scientific principles, Martin is full of remorse and shame. Although the islanders lionize him for ending the siege of plague, he feels that he has disgraced himself. Because of the contaminated experiment, no one can say for sure what may have abated the epidemic. The knowing pity of St. Hubert's best doctor is worse to Martin than condemnation (381).

Ultimately, however, medical research profits greatly from Martin's failure. Strongly motivated by humiliation and then by the loss of Max Gottlieb to senile dementia, Martin finally becomes an uncompromising and productive scientist. "Those beautiful long hours of search for truth" (403) prove to be a greater lure than a life of luxury and social respectability, a professional position of respect and authority, and a family. Martin and like-minded colleague Terry Wickett team up to take on the most exciting and challenging research work which either has ever known. At the end of the novel, Martin takes up residence in Wickett's retreat in the wilderness where the two can experience "the rapture of being allowed to work twenty-four hours a day without leaving an experiment at its juiciest moment" (426). In their humble laboratory in the forest, they can devote themselves completely to "pure" research— that is, they can be free from corrupting influences and from pressures to conduct "practical" research. And although some may see their move as the return of science to the monastery (427), Martin and Terry see it as the return of scientists to their proper function. They plan to allow other dedicated researchers to join them eventually but will have no dealings with anyone or any institution of lower scientific standards.

Martin and Terry's standards are, with some additions and adjustments, those of Max Gottlieb. The two proceed essentially as Gottlieb would have, not out of blind loyalty to him personally or for the sake of tradition but simply in agreement with his principles.

Most importantly, they have a very high standard for scientific integrity. Like Gottlieb, Arrowsmith and Wickett believe that scientists should consider the goal of their work to be the obtaining of reliable new data rather than the publishing of reports. That is, scientists should publish only verified results and should take credit for only that work which they have completed; but their first concern should be to learn the fundamental principles which govern the phenomena they observe. Their written reports should in no way be misleading about what has actually been proven. Medical science is not enriched by such imaginative literature as Almus Pickerbaugh's accounts of sighting the germ of epilepsy and two different germs of cancer. Martin and Terry, like Gottlieb, resist pressure from the Institute's administration to publish their results prematurely. Martin refuses to allow his incompletely tested "X Principle" to be used in less scrupulous researchers' projects, even after the director offers to double his salary and make him a department head if the joint projects succeed. He still does not give in when the assistant director tries to tempt him with the prospect of the awards and prizes, the social position, and the choice professorship that can be his if his discovery "really pans out" (308). Martin's work is not for sale, especially when it is not even finished.

Martin and Terry's ideas about cooperation and competition are not the popular ones, and they certainly contrast with those of Dr. Tubbs, the Institute's director. Interested in nothing but promoting the Institute, Tubbs first says, "Efficient universal *co-operation*—that's the thing in science today—the time of this silly, jealous, fumbling individual research has gone by" (308). Later, in a more desperate effort to get Martin to rush into publication, Tubbs says, "This is no longer an age of parochialism but of competition, in art and science just as much as in commerce—co-operation with your own group, but with those outside it, competition to the death!" (310). Late in the novel, Martin and Terry do collaborate very effectively, but only because the two have the same high standards for their work.

Only once does Martin feel that he is in competition with anyone else, and at that time Gottlieb teaches him a lesson in scientific sportsmanship. When a French researcher is the first to report a phenomenon that he and Martin have each discovered independently, Martin feels robbed of the acclaim for all his hard work. Gottlieb suggests that instead of pouting and trying to dispute the Frenchman's priority in the discovery, Martin should write a congratulatory letter and go back to work on his own research. Martin does so, planning to publish a report to corroborate his competitor's work and treat some points not yet covered. Says Gottlieb, "That is science: to work and not to care— too much—if somebody else gets the credit" (314).

One message in *Arrowsmith* is that dignity and courtesy should govern scientists' dealings with each other. Martin and his two friends believe that, as much as possible, researchers should remain aloof from the politics of the work place. They themselves keep too busy to take part in the intrigues that often beset the Institute. But when they feel called upon to speak their minds, they do so openly and clearly; they do not become involved in whispering campaigns. By contrast, other scientists at the Institute occupy themselves with slander, accusations of idea-stealing, factionalism, struggles for power, etc. Although Gottlieb and Wickett are not above insulting certain of their colleagues, they are above-board about it and truthful in what they say.

After all, scientific integrity also demands exactness and rigorous objectivity. Toward the end of the novel, the narrator says that Martin's world has become "cold, exact, austerely materialistic, bitter to those who founded their logic on impressions" (388). Martin has taken to heart Max Gottlieb's denouncement of all types of people who believe in unproven notions, including "pseudo-scientists," psychoanalysts and the people in the so-called social sciences, who "can only make guesses" (267-68). Skepticism is the guiding principle, and Martin has learned Gottlieb's "ultimate lesson of science, which is to wait and doubt" (15). He agrees with his teacher that there is nothing certain but the quantitative method (40). He has internalized the master's admonition, "Observe what you observe, and if it does violence to all the nice correct views of science— out they go!" (53). On the other hand, Martin has learned that an important component of objectivity is appreciating how little one knows. In addition, he has had the good example of Gustaf Sondelius, who did not "regard a difference of scientific opinion as an attack on his character" (335).

Complete objectivity is, of course, an unreachable goal for any human being; and the researcher has feelings just as everyone else does. From Gottlieb, Martin has heard that although the scientist is necessarily heartless in one sense and "lives in a cold, clear light," he [or she] is neither heartless nor cold in private (268). From Gottlieb's point of view, the scientist, who works and searches without "howling how he loves everybody," cares more deeply about the world than all the "Professional Optimists," who have no real idea what they are doing yet proclaim their altruism (268). Martin, whose professional passion has already been noted, certainly agrees that the coldness of the researcher does not have to mean a lack of feeling. He rejects one woman's comment, "The trouble with scientists is that they do not understand beauty. They are so cold" (312).

Martin's feeling for humanity, however, seems to diminish in proportion to his length of time in service to science. The narrator says of Martin on his first day as a full-time researcher, "Suddenly he loved humanity as he loved the decent, clean rows of test-tubes" (269). Close to the end of the novel, Terry Wickett, in apparent accord with Martin's sentiments, says of the monkeys he and Martin are using in experiments, "Why should we murder live-wires like them to save pasty-faced, big-bellied humans from pneumonia?" (404). He later affirms the "purity" of his and Martin's research by saying, "...we're not trying to solve anything for anybody but our own fool selves" (427). At the end of the novel, Martin is becoming "stronger and surer—and no doubt less human" (428).

When Gottlieb asserts that the scientist, fervent and "intensely religious" (267), is far from unfeeling, he refers to the scientist's feeling for research work; and Martin's professional zeal confirms his teacher's words. Gottlieb says that the desire to be a scientist is "a tangle of very [sic] obscure emotions, like mysticism, or wanting to write poetry" (267). As mentioned, the word *lyric* is used to describe Martin's feeling for his first original research. Several times in the novel, the awe and rapture felt by a scientist in the laboratory are likened to a religious experience. Martin's enthusiasm for his work is referred to as fanaticism.

Nevertheless, scientific discovery depends on knowledge much more than zeal. Martin learns from Wickett and Gottlieb that the dedicated scientist cannot in good conscience remain ignorant about anything related to his or her specialty. As Wickett says, "Science is supposed to mean Knowledge" (286). Albeit grudgingly at first, Martin accepts the responsibility to educate himself properly for his chosen career, even though his study and his work leave him little time for sleep. He learns to see his education and his research as "the work whose end is satisfying because there is never an end" (287).

As important as knowledge is, Martin knows that the researcher often has the help of good luck and coincidence. Martin stumbles, as it were, into his first two important findings in the laboratory. During the project which leads to his first publication, he tells his wife that most scientific discoveries are accidental and that no researcher, however great, can do more than "see the value of his chance results" (248).

Even so, being able to take advantage of good luck depends on the true scientist's insatiable desire to find things out. The narrator says that Martin makes his second accidental discovery because of his "one gift: curiosity whereby he saw nothing as ordinary" (295). Several times in the novel, the narrator pays tribute to Martin's perpetual desire to investigate. Martin's "wide-ranging, sniffing, snuffling, undignified, unself-dramatizing curiosity" is a "characteristic without which there can be no science" (280). Martin is compared to both a detective and a beagle.

In laboratory work, however, all luck, knowledge, and curiosity are of little use without the craftsmanship necessary in conducting experiments. In *Arrowsmith*, manual dexterity and ingenuity are shown to be very important components of this craftsmanship. Even as a student, Martin demonstrates a high degree of skill in bacteriological work, and late in the novel he demonstrates great competence in developing his own apparatus.

Gottlieb, noting Martin's early signs of technical ability, says, "Oh, there is an art in science—for a few" (39). It is also emphasized in the novel that patience and thoroughness belong to the craft. Martin learns to love "the beautiful dullness of long labors" (39); and when he is especially inspired, he does not notice the tediousness of bacteriological work. The value which he personally places on thoroughness is seen in his "prayer of the scientist," even if this statement of faith seems but an echo of Gottlieb's teaching: "God give me...freedom from haste. God give me a quiet and relentless anger against...all pretentious work and all work left slack and unfinished" (269). This feeling for the craft of research and the native ability to do the work well are perhaps what Gottlieb has in mind when he says, "To be a scientist is like being a Goethe: it is born in you" (268).

Throughout the novel, far more is said about what the medical scientist should *be* than about what he or she should or should not *do* in experimentation. Martin and Terry believe that the scientist should have complete freedom in subject matter and method of research. Their only stipulation is that there be a real investigation of something and not just a random collection of data and a naming of things. The narrator mentions Terry's "resentment, as great as Gottlieb's, of the morphological scientists who ticket things with the nicest little tickets, who name things and rename them and never analyze them" (279). As Martin matures as a scientist, he grows "daily more scornful toward the counters of paving stones, the renamers of species, the compilers of irrelevant data" (388). As for such practices as vivisection or human experimentation, Martin and Terry state no prohibitions. Both researchers use laboratory animals and are speechless with disgust for a prosperous physician who says, "I never have to kill any poor wee little beasties to get my knowledge!" (283). Martin's use of human subjects has already been treated in detail. It should be reiterated, however, that those who receive his experimental vaccine ask for it and stand an excellent chance of dying without it.

Just as Martin and Terry speak of no moral limits to honest science, so they mention no natural limits; but Max Gottlieb and the narrator bring the capabilities of science and medicine into question. When Martin is being celebrated as the savior of St. Hubert, the narrator adds a tentative disclaimer: "No one heeded a wry Scotch doctor, diligent but undramatic through the epidemic, who hinted that plagues have been known to slacken and cease without phage [Martin's vaccine]" (379). There is a further statement implied in the irony that Sondelius, the great soldier of preventive medicine and fighter of epidemics, is felled by the bite of one plague-carrying flea. Gottlieb raises serious doubt about the ultimate good of wholesale immunization against diseases and hence about humankind's ability to control nature. He fears that the human race may eventually become "so low in natural immunity that...a great plague...might wipe out the world entire" (121). He also speculates that the cost of freedom from disease would be intolerable overcrowding and famine (121). Martin apparently considers such matters too theoretical for his concern. At the end of the novel, he is happy just to be doing the work that he loves, whatever its eventual effect may be. He is content that ahead of him are "innumerous inquiries into chemotherapy and immunity; enough adventures to keep him busy for decades" (428).

While *Arrowsmith* may be considered the quintessential medical research novel in English and most of Martin Arrowsmith's opinions above are echoed again and again in this group of novels, these attitudes are by no means the last word. Some of the other protagonists' and narrators' views will now be presented in order to establish a consensus in the subgenre.

As one might assume, all of the novels indicate that the doctor should be knowledgeable and skillful and should take a scientific approach to the practice of medicine. That is, diagnoses should be based on the actual findings of the doctor's systematic investigations; treatments should be prescribed on the basis of the latest, most reliable information available. The doctor should depend on neither sudden inspiration nor tradition alone. A patient's comment to the protagonist in Irving Fineman's *Doctor Addams* expresses this idea very well: "I told Doctor Bird you were the only physician I knew who used his mind, not just his memory."[3] Richard Cameron in *The Undaunted* observes that most doctors, for all their stubborn individuality, are not independent thinkers as medical scientists.[4] The narrator, paraphrasing Cameron's thoughts, says, "Trained to accept this man's pronouncements on skin and another's on heart disease and another's on tuberculosis, they became followers who waited for a master's voice and then obeyed it" (229). On the other hand, Cameron notes a trend toward research-mindedness among physicians in the 1930s, saying that "a doctor is known these days by what he publishes and reads at medical meetings" (78). In many of the novels, and most notably in *Narkose, Semmelweis, der Retter der Mütter, The Cry and the Covenant*, and *Helfer der Menschheit*, the main character has to work—at least for a time—in a generally antiscientific or pseudo-scientific environment.[5] In such situations, the authors expose the unscientific attitudes or practices by setting them against the protagonist's standards. There are three novels, however, in which every physician is at least a respecter of science if not a researcher; an ideal, unified medical-scientific community is presented in Betina Ewerbeck's *Angela Koldewey*, W.B. Erlin's *Die Spur*, and Rudolf Daumann's *Patrouille gegen den Tod*.[6]

Objectivity, one of the most important requirements for scientific medical practice, has already been discussed in connection with Martin Arrowsmith. All of the other main characters, even if they do not always follow their own advice, would surely agree that the doctor needs to maintain objectivity. Many of them would say, however, that the doctor should basically be motivated by compassion. The central character's empathy with patients is especially stressed in *The Cry and the Covenant, Semmelweis, der Retter der Mütter, Angela Koldewey, Narkose*, and to a lesser extent, in other novels. On the other hand, several of the chief characters find out that strong personal attachment to or dislike of the patient can cause problems. For example, Josef Zeppichmann in *The Fire and the Wood* and Georg Letham in *Georg Letham, Arzt und Mörder* each fall in love with a patient, and Martin Bertram in *Viele sind berufen* is strongly tempted to kill a patient who could reveal certain information that would destroy Bertram's career.[7]

Given the protagonists' agreement that the doctor should proceed scientifically and objectively, one might expect them to be honest and open with their patients. As a rule they are, but some of them encounter a special case which seems to justify their being less than forthright. For example, Martin Bertram in *Viele sind berufen* administers a series of placebo injections to allow a terminally ill patient to die with courage and in peace. Richard Cameron in *The Undaunted* sustains a victim of pernicious anemia, who is also an adamant vegetarian, by surreptitiously feeding him a liver extract. In the subgenre there are also examples of deception or the withholding of information for less honorable reasons, but overall the medical research novel clearly advocates the open and honest practice of medicine, even when the patient would prefer hocus-pocus to real treatment. As the narrator of *Helfer der Menschheit* says, "...vor sich selbst und seinem Gewissen musste man zuerst bestehn" (67). In *The Cry and the Covenant*, Ignaz Philipp Semmelweis and his friends denounce the "mantle of mysticism" with which the medical profession surrounds itself, and the author clearly intends this criticism of medicine in the Austro-Hungarian Empire of the nineteenth century to be applied to twentieth-century America as well:

> ...we draw on the ancient priestcraft. We dress mysteriously, we have our special costumes. We have our own language, our own magic gibberish. We have had laws passed to protect the omniscience to which we pretend. We protect one another like members of a priestly fraternity. We foster the belief that we are a mystery. The hold we have on people is their own fear, pain, terror, and ignorance. (209)

Although the general populace is no longer as ignorant of medical matters as it was in the mid-nineteenth century, the present high degree of specialization helps modern medicine maintain a certain aura and mystique. Many people in real life and in fiction consider medicine overspecialized. The implied consensus in medical research novels is that while the doctor may eventually have to specialize, he or she needs a broad base of experience; and in any case, very narrow specialization is not good. Of the seventeen central characters studied here, eleven either serve as general practitioners at some time or benefit from diversified medical experience.[8] Only Richard Cameron, though once a country doctor himself, speaks in favor of specialization in the practice of medicine. Cameron does not believe that the passing of the old family doctor should be mourned any more than the passing of hansom cabs and the covered wagon (296). He says, "Whether we approve or not, society is being mechanized and the medical profession, being a part of society, must share the process" (296-297). On the other side of the argument, Martin Bertram in *Viele sind berufen* seems to agree with his partner Genia's denunciation of overly specialized medicine. She maintains that an unlucky patient choosing the wrong kind of specialist could die by following the doctor's advice (124). In *Doctor Addams* there is mention of the abuses that come from overspecialization: fee-splitting and passing the patient among specialists "to the extent of his needs and means" (57). Alex Addams, considered an anomaly because of his diverse areas of expertise, deplores "metropolitan practice, its venal competition, its unscrupulous exploitation of human ailment, its pretentious specialization of impotent knowledge" (136).

Those doctors who exploit the ill or otherwise treat the practice of medicine as a business draw some of the worst criticism, direct or implied. Dr. Charles Jackson in *Narkose*, for example, is distinguished from the downright quacks only by his education. Though a knowledgeable and capable doctor, Jackson is a schemer who lays claim to the protagonist's discovery and often gives patients what they think they want rather than what is medically sound. In *The Fire and the Wood* a careless comment by Josef Zeppichmann causes a colleague to ask accusingly, "...do you think it's a doctor's business to give sick people what they want?" and "Do you mean you'll only use your knowledge of healing for people who pay you?" (128). In *The Undaunted*, Richard Cameron himself becomes a patient and criticizes a hospital for being "too business-like, too impersonal, too efficient" (225). The narrator says, paraphrasing Cameron's thoughts, "This hospital was like a factory: it too was dedicated to mass production" (225).

In one way or another, every author shows that the needs of the patient should be the medical profession's primary concern and that the patient should be treated as a person. During his hospitalization, Cameron resents being in the care of specialists interested not in him but in the experience he provides them. Josef Zeppichmann is criticized for being one of those doctors who "just doesn't notice the patients at all" (36). His patients are "merely specimens of dilapidation for him to practise on" (36). By the end of the novel, however, he has had a complete change of heart. The narrator-protagonist of *Georg Letham, Arzt und Mörder* says frankly, "Die Krankheiten interessierten mich, die Kranken interessierten mich nicht" (13); but his feelings for one patient make him realize that saving human lives is the ultimate reason for medical research. Many of the main characters, of course, are by nature empathetic with patients all along. Robert Koch in *Helfer der Menschheit* is said to have what every doctor needs, an "Übermass an Liebe und Preisgabe" (55). And as already noted indirectly, Ignaz Philipp Semmelweis in *The Cry and the Covenant* and *Retter der Mütter*, William T.G. Morton in *Narkose*, and Angela Koldewey in the novel of the same name exemplify the compassionate physician.

Some of the main characters believe that the doctor should care for more than the physical needs of patients; that is, since body, mind, and soul all work together, the doctor should attempt to treat the whole person. To calm fearful patients, Angela Koldewey spends much more time talking to them than her superiors deem professionally correct. Martin Bertram thinks that doctors should do more to help patients face death. In this and other matters, he says, they could learn a lot from poets; but he realizes that those people who most need poets have no time for them (234). Walter Töpfer in *Die Trennung* feels professionally obligated to lighten the emotional burdens of his patients whenever possible.[9] To brighten one patient's emotional outlook, Semmelweis in *The Cry and the Covenant* delivers a message to her husband in prison. However, most of the protagonists who are involved in medical practice have either no desire or no time to minister to the spirit while mending the body.

But regardless of such considerations, healing alone does not give complete professional satisfaction. Robert Koch is never altogether satisfied with doctoring. His research is motivated in part by his realization of how often the doctor cannot help (84). Walter Töpfer also takes up research because of his frustrations as a doctor. Alfried Kalsten in *Patrouille gegen den Tod* wants to combat deadly diseases directly— through research—to keep as many people as possible from dying before their time. He wants to find out "wie man diesen blöden, dummen Zufallstod aus der Welt jagen könnte" (34). Even though some of the main characters have less altruistic reasons for getting involved with experimentation, all have similar feelings about their effectiveness in research and inadequacy in medical practice only.

Most protagonists are also more stimulated by the laboratory work than the clinical work. The usual pattern is that the chief character becomes so fascinated with research in general and so committed to one or more specific research goals that everything else becomes secondary in importance, at least temporarily. Eventually, most of the central characters either give up medical practice in favor of full-time research or wish that they could.

Preoccupation with research does not necessarily preclude continued medical practice of some kind, but very few of the main characters can maintain a dual career without eventually encountering some important conflict in the interests of science and medicine. As a group, the protagonists have conflicts concerning time, responsibilities, and ideas about the purpose of research.

The most obvious problem for a person interested in both research and medical practice is that the two pursuits may compete for his or her time. Regardless of the physician's commitment to be available to render medical assistance at any time, a research project may come to demand full-time attention. This dilemma is described well by the narrator of *Doctor Addams*, who says that the protagonist sometimes "wished for a dual personality, so that one of him might go about his true scientific concerns while the other attended this business of giving comfort or cure, of dividing again and again the loaves and fishes of his mind and spirit" (59).

As is shown so clearly in *Arrowsmith*, science and medicine have different concerns and responsibilities. While scientists promise eventual benefit to the human race from the knowledge they acquire, they are not necessarily concerned with the immediate welfare of individuals.

Doctors, on the other hand, are bound by an oath to try to heal and mend people presently in need, whether or not this work interferes with someone's research. In certain situations which will be presented later, the doctor-researcher must choose allegiance to either medicine or science but cannot remain completely faithful to both.

It follows, then, that the scientific and the medical establishments often have different expectations for research. Although doctors would like to see new cures and new means of alleviating pain and discomfort, contemporary research may not produce usable results for some time. Alex Addams makes the point that scientists often serve not their own generation but a generation to come (81). Moreover, a particular research project may yield a bit of medical knowledge which, though important, appears small and insignificant in itself. Thinking along these lines, Henry Baker in *Medical Meeting* is struck by his colleagues' tendency to call a completed project a "piece of work."[10] "But," says the narrator, paraphrasing Baker's thoughts, "that was all it was: a piece of truth" (108).

Trying to achieve real depth of knowledge, the medical scientist may become a very narrow specialist, regardless of what he or she feels about excessive specialization in medical practice. This tendency is not necessarily a bad thing, however. To Hans Lennhoff of *Die Spur*, the word *Spezialist* has no negative connotation: "In bestimmten Fällen kam man ohne Spezialisten gar nicht aus—ohne jene Leute, die ihr Blickfeld ganz bewusst verengten,...weil es dadurch an Tiefenschärfe gewann" (161). Besides, many of the protagonists, because of the uninhibited nature of their intellect, become surprisingly diversified in their research careers.

Regardless of their scope, all of the main characters have to decide whether medicine or science should receive the emphasis in their work. Understandably, they are not completely agreed on the proper function of research. Alex Addams, like Martin Arrowsmith and friends, believes that no pragmatic demands should be made of experimentation:

...the itch to know this world and to express that knowledge comes, must come, before the use, the application of that knowledge; and radicals who sneer and cry "escapist," when they see a man single-mindedly engaged in the search for knowledge, are endangering the continuance of civilization, stopping its life blood at the source. (104)

The central characters of the other novels would probably agree with Addams and Arrowsmith in theory; however, in practice, they align themselves with Semmelweis, who says in *The Cry and the Covenant*, "Knowledge for the sake of knowledge isn't enough" (120). For him, the true value is in the medical use of any knowledge acquired. Of all the chief characters, only Addams and Arrowsmith are involved in "pure" research, that is, in projects which have no direct connection to the cure of specific diseases or to any new medical procedure.

Whether involved in "pure" or "practical" research, most of the protagonists feel about their profession as Alex Addams does: it is "the noblest work" (9). In modern medical science Addams sees "man verging on the realization of his great powers for good; something close to divinity" (453). In most of the novels, the search for knowledge is deemed a quest for truth and regarded as having an epic or almost holy quality.

All of the main characters would surely agree, at least in theory, that to be successful in the pursuit of knowledge, the researcher must be clear-headed, factual, and objective, just as the doctor should be. However, Koldewey, Morton, and Semmelweis are so motivated by compassion that they have difficulty in mentally dissociating facts from the suffering people to whom they pertain. The rest of the central characters know that the true scientist, who must work with proofs rather than assumptions, must be as exact and as impartial toward data as a mathematician. Robert Koch in *Helfer der Menschheit* is very self-critical and "rücksichtslos" in his judgment of his or anyone else's theories (117), and most of his counterparts in the other novels are also shown to have these qualities. Alex Addams agrees with his most influential teacher that an important ingredient of impartiality is humility. Humility is so important, in fact, that it is one of the two "scientific virtues" (87).

Most of the chief characters believe that unprejudiced research also requires an even greater detachment than is desirable in medical practice. Josef Zeppichmann, using a human experimental subject, warns himself that "the patient's private interest" blocks "the view of one's objective" (105). And in *Medical Meeting* a colleague of Henry Baker's says emphatically, "There is no place for the human angle in medical research. It cannot enter in. Henry knows that" (124). Even while maintaining a concern for his patients as people, Baker tries to consider and present his information about them in a disinterested manner.

Not all of the other protagonists are like Baker in this regard: an observable phenomenon in the career of many of the doctor-researchers is a loss of touch with the immediate medical needs of individuals, at least temporarily. Martin Bertram finds at one point that he can hardly tolerate his hospital duties because he is impatient to get back to work on his project. Even Walter Töpfer in *Die Trennung*, who undertakes his research because he wants to do more for his patients, becomes so absorbed in his laboratory work that he starts to think in terms of medical statistics rather than suffering human beings: "Er hatte sich tief verändert. Er hatte diesen neuen Weg eingeschlagen im Gedanken und Gefühl für die Leiden der Kranken—und nun sah er nichts mehr als Fälle, Phänomene und Prozesse" (130). Alex Addams, who in the first part of the novel is a practicing physician as well as a researcher and lecturer, suddenly realizes one day how his thinking, even on medical topics, has been affected by his research. His reaction to a student's question is notable: "It was startling to hear the word 'patient'; he had been thinking of tissues and electric potentials, of a process, not of a human being" (48). Joseph Zeppichmann, whose unfortunate attitude toward patients in general has already been noted, considers terminal tuberculars to be expendable material for scientific use. He administers his experimental drug to a young woman without first telling her that it may kill her in the process of killing the target bacilli. Georg Letham, seeing a chance to add an especially good case study to the data in his group's experiment, purposely allows a mosquito carrying the yellow fever virus to bite the pregnant wife of the dying project leader. He hopes to determine whether a mother can transmit yellow fever to her baby during pregnancy. Although Letham suffers pangs of conscience and knows that he will be guilty of murder if the woman or the baby dies, he cannot say that he would act differently if faced with the same type of situation again (423).

Richard Cameron has a unique moral problem. In the interests of both science and medicine, he deceives and exploits a strict vegetarian who would rather die than ingest the only cure for his disease. At first Cameron maintains that this disagreeable man's serving unknowingly and unwillingly as a test case is "the only way he'll ever pay for the trouble he's been to the world in general" (158); but later, Cameron respects this patient's right to die for his principles.

Fortunately, research work does not make all of the protagonists begin to treat patients like laboratory animals, nor does it completely desensitize any of the doctor-scientists.[11] In some cases, the net effect of the research work is to make the main character more aware of patients as people. For example, Walter Töpfer says that he has missed his contact with patients during the most intensive period of his research. He wants to remain a full-time researcher only long enough to finish the particular work he has started. "Ich brauche wieder Menschen," he says; all of his privations and exertions have been "nur für Menschen" (224). Angela Koldewey's research into case histories makes her feel a personal acquaintance with patients' life situations. Her mind forms pictures of the people whose information is on file. Semmelweis is at times driven only by the thought of all the mothers and newborn babies who will suffer and die until puerperal fever is ended. His research work, dissecting hundreds of cadavers, makes him all the more concerned about his patients as living human beings. Furthermore, he discovers that women in his maternity ward contract childbed fever primarily from the frequent and unsanitary pelvic examinations conducted by doctors and medical students, who tend to regard the patients strictly as maternity case studies. As indicated earlier, some of Semmelweis' counterparts in other novels even develop personal relationships with patients because of their research. In four cases, a patient who is also the subject of an experiment becomes a source of special concern and pride.[12]

None of the central characters is, on balance, inhuman or unscrupulous. Notwithstanding a statement by Georg Letham that there are no moral obstacles for the researcher in today's world (24), all of the protagonists either work within some sort of moral constraints or come to regret not having done so. In various ways, the subgenre reveals a universal code of scientific ethics, permissive though it may seem. This code does not, for example, prohibit vivisection or even the use of human subjects in experimentation. However, it does disallow unnecessary cruelty to laboratory animals, as is mentioned in *Viele sind berufen*, and the use of unwilling or unwitting persons in experimentation, as seen in *The Undaunted, The Fire and the Wood* and *Georg Letham, Arzt und Mörder*.[13]

In *Viele sind berufen* there is also a forceful demand for moral responsibility in research. Martin Bertram and his friend Wendemuth are outraged when a colleague announces that he will attempt to reestablish the circulation of blood in the severed head of an executed murderer. Bertram objects to the use of a human body for something more like a freak show than an experiment for medical science. Wendemuth, otherwise the voice of pure science, rages against the indulgence of whim and mere idle curiosity: "Des Satans seid ihr mit eurer verfluchten Neugierde!" (363). Reminiscent of Martin Arrowsmith but more extreme, Wendemuth upholds the banner of relevant data collection, saying, "Welch menschenfresserischen Moloch haben diese Gesichtslosen aus der Wissenschaft gemacht!" (364).

Unfortunately, bizarre and pointless experimentation is not the worst thing on the scientific horizon: the use of scientific knowledge for evil purposes is a recurrent topic. In *Doctor Addams* and *The Undaunted* there is some general discussion of this subject, and in *Narkose* there is mention of moral opposition to dentists' use of ether because of the possibility that women under anesthesia will be sexually molested. Other novels deal with more than theoretical possibilities. Georg Letham, doctor and murderer, gives his wife a lethal injection of the scarlet fever toxin which he has isolated and concentrated. A nurse in *Die Trennung* injects a patient with live tetanus germs from Walter Töpfer's culture in the clinic's laboratory. In *Die japanische Pest* the Japanese military plans to conquer the world with a new type of plague.[14] The unsuspecting Fritz Wieser has been instrumental in developing the immunization that would protect the aggressors.

While admitting that science can and sometimes does place great power in evil hands, the main characters as a group would agree that science cannot be held responsible for the misuse of its discoveries. Among the novels which treat the subject directly, the consensus is that the fault for any misuse of scientific knowledge lies with only those who apply that knowledge in some immoral way; after all, it makes no sense to fault the desire to know more about the physical world. Alex Addams places the blame "not on science but on those who provided occasions for the use of science for evil instead of for good" (91). A person who finds science guilty, he says, "might just as logically censure the invention of the kitchen knife because men [have] sometimes employed that instrument to commit murder" (91). Richard Cameron echoes Addams' opinion: "If people haven't got sense enough to use scientific discoveries decently, that isn't the fault of the scientist" (167).

Indeed, much of the discussion of ethics concerns the researcher's loyalty to the pursuit of knowledge. For example, in *Viele sind berufen* genuine scientists are said to be involved in research because of an interest in furthering science rather than in making money or in building a career (222-223). In *The Undaunted* those considered the true professionals are dedicated to learning rather than to making money; they are unselfish with the knowledge they gain and are "not intolerant of other men in search of truth" (197).

This call for tolerance is only one of several indications of a code of conduct governing the scientist's professional relationships. In *The Undaunted* the "real" scientists—the models of professionalism—are those who refrain from both pettiness and involvement in "entangling alliances" and who are not prone to the prejudices and the jealousies that often seem to dictate the actions of most of their colleagues (196). In *Die Spur* Hans Lennhoff and his superior agree that a person who does not act out of concern for the general welfare is not involved in real *scientific* research at all: "Wissenschaftliche Forschung, die nicht die Wohlfahrt aller im Auge hat, bedeutet einen Widerspruch in sich selbst" (185). The director of the research institute says, and Lennhoff obviously agrees, that there is no room in science for egotism and jealousy: "Es gibt nichts Beschämenderes als eine von egoistischen Gesichtspunkten bestimmte Wissenschaft. Dasselbe gilt für die wissenschaftliche Eifersüchtelei" (185). In *Die Spur* and in other novels as well, the model scientists are possessed of the basic, all-inclusive virtue of gentlemanliness, which is essentially good sportsmanship and courtesy.

In *Doctor Addams* the first of the two "scientific virtues" is integrity, a combination of good sportsmanship, self-respect, and a feeling of responsibility to the truth (87). In this and other novels there are many specific examples of integrity, such as Addams' opposition to premature publicity of his research, Addams' and his colleague Hans Kohn's feeling that a scientist should report reservations as well as results, Hans Lennhoff's sharing credit with his assistant on their published report, Henry Baker's stripping his oral presentation of any statements that may evoke sympathy or seem to solicit praise, and Richard Cameron's refusal of a handsomely paying job endorsing second-rate products for a pharmaceutical company.

The integrity of the individual researcher either as part of a group or in competition with a collective is also an important theme in the subgenre. Despite admonitions against narrowness and egotism, the novels show that the great scientist, like the greats in other fields of endeavor, is a staunchly independent spirit. The majority of the protagonists do not normally collaborate with other researchers, and in some cases they are competing with groups of researchers who have superior resources. Some of the main characters have doubts that they can succeed in solving a particular problem that has eluded even some of the "big names" in research, but they continue to work doggedly toward their goal. One example is Martin Bertram, who becomes encouraged by his friend Wendemuth's reminder that almost all really important discoveries have been made by "kleinen Leuten" and that one does not hear of an important contribution being made by a collective of twenty researchers (448-49). Some of the central characters do collaborate effectively with one or two other scientists, but their individual genius asserts itself. The case of Hans Lennhoff makes an important statement: part of an international effort to defeat a new disease, he is the first to identify the microbe because he does not follow the advice of his colleagues.

Medical research novels offer many ideas about what it takes—in addition to belief in oneself—to be a really good medical scientist, and perhaps the most obvious requirement is dedication and devotion to research. Ironically, this attachment is most often described in terms of something overwhelming and uncontrollable rather than something cerebral and steady. It is repeatedly likened to erotic love or to fanaticism. Alex Addams feels that what makes a good scientist is "an indescribable passion for the act of research" (166). Georg Letham echoes this feeling: "Forschertätigkeit ist ein Glück, das an Tiefe nur dem Lieben (nicht dem Geliebtwerden!) zu vergleichen ist" (331). Letham also mentions the "gewaltige Befriedigung" of positive research results (26). In *Die Spur*, Hans Lennhoff's superior says that the specially gifted researcher has a feeling for his or her work which is "die allerletzte blinde Besessenheit" (103). In *Medical Meeting* Henry Baker's project is called his "obsession" (31). The word *Fanatismus* is used in both *Helfer der Menschheit* (233) and *Die Trennung* (175) to describe the chief character's commitment to his research work. Several references to the fanaticism of the "pure" scientist are made in *The Undaunted*; and one such researcher, Dr. Montagu, is also called a "crusader" (125) and a "burning-eyed zealot" (129). However, a very marked distinction is made between Montagu and the protagonist Cameron, who is "an adventurer—not a crusader, not a fanatic, not an inhuman driver of lesser men, but a man who might better have lived in the sixteenth century and been a buccaneer in his Queen's service" (137).

Devotion to research is recurringly expressed with military imagery and emphasis on loyalty, courage, and the fighting spirit. Indeed, at the height of research activity, most of the main characters live much like soldiers in a battle zone. In *Die Japanische Pest* Fritz Wieser's hazardous duty at a remote military outpost demands "Mut" among other things (9). In *Zwischenfall in Lohwinckel* researchers are hailed as "Kämpfer" (319). In *Helfer der Menschheit* the reader's attention is called to the need for soldierly valor (283) and "Treue zum Werk" (307). "Treue" is also mentioned as a necessary quality of the successful researcher in *Viele sind berufen* (475).

Every main character shows great perseverance, and this quality is given special recognition in three novels. Martin Bertram in *Viele sind berufen* says that two rules for the researcher's success are "Beharrlichkeit zeigen" and "Konsequent bleiben" (475). In *Medical Meeting* the narrator emphasizes Henry Baker's stubborn pursuit of an idea (24-25). In *Zwischenfall in Lohwinckel* dedicated researchers are called, among other things, "Leute, die lieber verrecken, als vom Gedanken ablassen" (319).

Such dedication inevitably means sacrifice, as every novel in the subgenre shows. Two central characters in particular demonstrate a conscious awareness of this fact. Robert Koch knows that there can be no great accomplishment without "Preisgabe" (233). Georg Letham gives a poignant enumeration of the specific costs of the researcher's dedication:

Alle Nachtwachen, alle gewissenhaften, in die Tiefe eindringenden Studien, alle Stunden des nagenden Zweifels und der Beunruhigung, alle Unkosten an Geld, alle für Versuche angewandte Zeit, was der Forscher mit dem Verzicht auf den gesellschaftlichen Verkehr, die Lektüre von Romanen, den Besuch von Theater und Konzerten, vor allem durch den Verzicht auf das wirklich intensive geistige Zusammenleben im Kreise seiner Familie bezahlt hat.... (26)

Some of the researchers—Letham included—also jeopardize their health or even their lives for the sake of their research.[15]

In almost every novel, the protagonist's devotion to medical science is at some point severely tested. Most of the chief characters have times of doubt about whether the gain from their work is worth the costs. In cases where their results are greeted with indifference or ingratitude, they wonder if humanity deserves the hard-won benefits of medical research. However, the researchers feel compelled to complete their work for their own satisfaction and, to varying degrees, for the sake of appreciative beneficiaries.

Richard Cameron, many of whose severely anemic patients complain about having to eat liver to stay alive, often wonders at their thanklessness. He also wonders at all people's small capacity for faith. He is saved from bewilderment, however, by his sense of humor. Besides, his work leaves him no time for further "fruitless speculation" about the human race (151).

Ignaz Philipp Semmelweis, already feeling defeated by the medical community's resistance to his simple doctrine of hospital sanitation, is on one occasion in *The Cry and the Covenant* jeered by some of the very women whose lives he has worked so hard to save. These women, insulted by the Hungarian doctor's and his staff's careful handwashings before and after each pelvic examination, exult when he is dismissed from the hospital. For a short time, Semmelweis feels that the women deserve to die, but he soon forgives them due to their ignorance.

William T.G. Morton becomes bitter when he cannot establish his priority in the surgical application of ether and cannot keep others from siphoning off his rightful profits from his discovery. To add more injury, there is a significant movement to ban the use of ether on moral grounds. At this point, Morton begins to feel that the human race is not worthy of any escape from pain. At bottom, however, Morton feels that the sad human creature is more to be pitied than condemned.

Walter Töpfer asks himself why he has sacrificed married life in order to provide a cure for ugly, unknown, unimportant sick people who mean nothing to him (176). Even so, he keeps working to complete his project.

In the final analysis, of course, all of the central characters feel that any success in their quest for knowledge is worth the price. Not one would disagree with Letham's statement that every deprivation "ist (für den Augenblick) reichlich abgegolten durch das Gefühl des Wissens, der Auflösung eines Rätsels, der Bereicherung der menschlichen Macht über die Dinge" (26).

The medical researcher's quest requires more than desire and dedication, of course; every novel indicates the great importance of the scientist's innate mental faculties. Each of the main characters is, if not downright brilliant, at least able to acquire, sort, store, and combine vast amounts of information and to apply the pertinent data to particular problems. Each also has great power of concentration. Quick decisiveness, though not usually associated with research work, becomes especially important in Fritz Wieser's and Alfried Kalsten's projects. But perhaps the most important mental trait for all of the protagonists is an insatiable curiosity, which several narrators point out specifically and all authors show in action.

The mental activities of the scientist are shown to be like those of the artist. There is a creative drive which attracts doctors to research in the first place and helps them reach their goals. The best researchers, says the narrator in *Die Spur*, are willing to try even what seems unlikely to produce results; they have "Phantasie" (209) and allow themselves to follow their "Intuition" (181). These qualities are mentioned specifically in other German novels also and are demonstrated in many of the novels of both languages.

Coincidence and sheer blind luck help, too, as most of the central characters would freely admit. All of them, however, are well prepared to take advantage of good fortune. They are always hard at work when a beneficial coincidence occurs, and a lucky break for them is only the beginning of more hard work. Moreover, without the curiosity and intuition stressed above, the researcher would perhaps fail to follow up the leads which he or she discovers accidently. In *Helfer der Menschheit* special care is taken to represent a proper balance in the process of scientific discovery. The narrator says, "Aber nicht mit romantischen Empfindungen geht man ans Werk, um auf Unvermutetes zu stossen und sich überraschen zu lassen, sondern wissenschaftlich nüchtern, zielbewusst und gewillt, alle erahnten Geheimnisse zu klären" (200).

The researcher must also be a craftsman in every way in addition to being a hard-working scientific thinker and a dreamer. Without craftsmanship, he or she, however brilliant or lucky, could make neither inspirations nor logical deductions bear fruit in the laboratory. The scientist must be precise and demanding of accuracy, unadorned facts and irrefutable proof. The medical researcher is typically depicted as clear and concise in thought and word, and some of the novels note that these qualities make his or her language a thing of beauty. Expressed physically, precision requires great manual dexterity, especially in the bacteriological laboratory; and almost all of the main characters are especially skilled in this way. The craftsman, and therefore the true scientist, is also patient and thorough. In some cases, the chief character must have a high tolerance for tedium, which means much physical as well as emotional endurance. As for thoroughness, the statement of the subgenre is well made by Martin Bertram's antipathy to "halbfertige und hingeschleuderte Arbeit" (347). In many of the other novels, too, it is explicitly observed that the researcher's work on a project is not complete until all reasonable doubts about the validity of the results can be satisfied. A scientific discovery must be judged not by the brilliance of the inspiration but by the impeccability of the proof.

Violations of this principle of thoroughness are nonetheless justified in two novels, but in both instances there is an urgent need to act and only one known remedy for a grave problem. In *Medical Meeting* Henry Baker administers his insufficiently tested tuberculostat to his dying daughter. He must then live with the guilt of having caused the girl's deafness by giving her too large a dosage. In *Patrouille gegen den Tod* a quickly developed drug, tested on only two people, is given without reservation to hundreds of thousands of Africans to check the rapid spread of a deadly new disease. In this case, the new drug is not only perfectly effective but also without side effects. It should be noted, however, that this novel is utopian, as indicated by its subtitle.

It has been seen that the protagonists and others have definite standards for science and place certain ethical limits on medical research. The natural limitations of medical science are also discussed in some novels. These constraints come from four sources: the world's hostility toward science, the human nature of those who conduct research and those who apply scientific knowledge, the shortcomings of scientific perception, and the power of nature.

Several of the novels indicate the world's hostility toward science. In particular, the four biographical novels, set in the early days of modern medical research, show the protagonists' struggles against anti-scientific attitudes. *Arrowsmith* and *The Undaunted,* set in more recent times, make reference to moral opposition to the use of living animals and humans in research; they also show how science is misunderstood by the general populace. In *Doctor Addams* the father and a colleague of the main character voice popular concerns about the misuse of science's powers. But nowhere is such general misunderstanding and distrust of the scientist better illustrated than in *Zwischenfall in Lohwinckel,* whose main character feels the opposition of the whole town.

The human frailties of scientists give science opposition from within as well. This point is an important theme in *The Undaunted.* Sandy Farquhar, a radiologist whose philosophy is in harmony with Richard Cameron's and the narrator's, thinks that science's achievements thus far have been "pitifully insignificant...compared with what might have been done" if people, particularly scientists, "could only work together, face things squarely as they were, set reason a guard over their conduct" (196-197). In *The Undaunted* and other novels as well, scientists' egos are shown to obstruct scientific progress.

Even at their most objective and reasonable, scientists do not have all the cures for humanity's ills. The point is made in *Viele sind berufen* and *Patrouille gegen den Tod* that dying people are in need of something more than what science and medicine can give them. During a short period of intense philosophical searching, Richard Cameron finds science inadequate to tell him what he wants to know about life: "Science was concerned with *How*, not *Why*" (292). Alex Addams' very religious colleague, Francis MacBride, suggests that science may have outlived its usefulness because it is doing nothing for the human spirit: "If science is not strengthening us morally maybe we'd better give it up" (139). Addams himself, from a completely different point of view, indicates that scientific perception is not completely adequate because it is necessarily limited in scope. He says that the isolated scientific truth about any phenomenon is only one truth: "...there is also another truth...which scientists do not know and that is the complex truth, the truth which is not abstracted and isolated from the complex and equivocal reality" (127). He suggests that perhaps the "unscientific practitioner" has this latter truth (127). Reasoning as Addams does, Cameron believes that medical research confined to the laboratory and not combined with clinical observation cannot provide reliable answers.

Science's ultimate power over nature is perennially in question, and the works in general deal honestly with this issue. Every one of the central characters knows from clinical experience how often medical science fails patients because doctors have not learned enough. In several instances, researchers frankly admit medical science's limitations. In *The Cry and the Covenant* Semmelweis in the 1840s says, "We are pitifully ignorant" (119). In *Patrouille gegen den Tod* biologist Robert Dobbertin reminds Alfried Kalsten of how ineffective medical science is in the fight against disease-causing microbes because researchers in the 1930s still know so little about the secret of life (57). Dobbertin has fears about future widespread epidemics, which bring to mind the theories of Max Gottlieb. Nikolas Persenthein in *Zwischenfall in Lohwinckel* believes that medical science's whole approach to the maintenance of health is entirely wrong. His radical idea is that doctors and researchers cannot protect anyone against health hazards except by building up the person's constitution with proper diet and systematically exposing him or her to the dangers. The person's *Disposition*, he thinks, will then adjust accordingly (21-22). Georg Letham believes in science no more than he believes in any other ideals. He has no confidence in the ability of science to make any lasting and significant changes in the order of things. Humanity can never triumph over nature, he says, because the human being is merely one of nature's experiments (179). Richard Cameron, in a negative frame of mind, wonders if any doctor accomplishes "anything beyond prolonging the time in which people might suffer and be unhappy" (283). He feels that he is, in effect, saving his patients from anemia so that they can die from something else. These same ideas are expressed in *Die Spur*, though not endorsed by the protagonist. A colleague of Hans Lennhoff's voices the popular opinion that the longer life expectancy achieved by medical science is not, on balance, a good thing (132). Besides, he says, medical research appears futile because there is a new disease to take the place of every one that is conquered (132-133). Indeed, Lennhoff, Fritz Wieser, and Alfried Kalsten each combat a newly discovered disease.

However, despite all the negatives, the main characters are all either basically optimistic about the capabilities of medicine and science or else usually content to ignore questions about the ultimate futility of medical research. Alex Addams, unshaken by the political fomentation which threatens the institute for which he works and unaffected by some people's serious doubts about science's ability to save humanity from itself, reaffirms his "faith in science and in freedom" (389). Robert Koch, portrayed in *Helfer der Menschheit* as a great white hunter of microbiological trophies, sees no limit to what science can do in conquering diseases. The narrator describes his hero's and the world's great optimism after Koch has developed his tuberculin: "Die furchtbarste Seuche ist heilbar! Bald sind es alle! So hat der Meister gesagt" (257). Koch's main concern, besides helping humanity with his knowledge and skills, is keeping the work challenging enough. In *The Undaunted* the feeling about the future of science is, as one might guess from the title, optimistic in the face of many difficulties. Cameron's friend Sandy Farquhar feels sure that science, despite the modern world's hostility toward it, will continue to achieve great things. In *Die Spur* Hans Lennhoff ignores skeptical remarks about medical science and works all the harder to conquer the particular disease that has captivated his attention. He is quite satisfied that medicine research will never run out of problems to solve. And Georg Letham, despite his general pessimism, participates in the beginning of what appears to be the final triumph over yellow fever and malaria.

The novels show medical researchers to be a very special breed of people. On the whole, they are independent, curious, creative, intelligent, intuitive but mentally disciplined, determined, courageous, honest, fair-minded, usually objective and sometimes lucky. They are hard-working, conscientious, and highly skilled craftsmen. As such, they must be painstakingly thorough and patient as well as passionate. These fictional medical researchers, like those in real life, combine the traits and talents of the doctor and the scientist.

The union of science and medicine, however, creates conflicts; and because of these conflicts, the conscientious physician actively pursuing scientific knowledge typically undergoes changes, at least temporary ones. In fact, most of the chief characters eventually leave medical practice to take up medical research full time if they can. They find the experimentation or exploration more stimulating than the clinical work and would rather try to help great numbers of people in the future than resign themselves to providing cure or comfort to comparatively few people. Thus concerned with statistics and the long term and dedicated to the ideal of scientific objectivity, most of the central characters show a tendency toward less sensitivity to the individual patient. On the other hand, some of them, because of their research work, become more aware of their patients as individuals. Furthermore, the great majority work exclusively on very "practical" projects.

For most of the protagonists, conducting medical research means adopting the ethics of science, which in some cases differ from those of medicine. In general, loyalty to the search for knowledge is valued above self-interest and immediate concerns of all other individuals. In *relevant* experimentation, exposing animals or even humans to extra medical risks is condoned, so long as the human subjects are willing and neither they nor the animals are caused unnecessary suffering. For purposes of data collection, withholding treatment that is merely presumed—but not yet proven—safe and effective is not only justified but demanded; but for humanitarian purposes, administering such treatment is sanctioned in extreme emergencies in two novels. For medical scientists as for anyone else, the overall guides for conduct are responsibility and integrity. Regarding responsibility, however, the consensus is that researchers acting in the best interests of science need not take the blame for others' misuse of their discoveries.

As might be expected, most of the main characters are generally quite optimistic about the present and future capabilities of their profession. However, in several novels, certain limitations of medical science are recognized. The fictional researchers are, of course, aware that their craft will never produce any panaceas because it cannot address all human needs. And even in their own sphere of influence, medical scientists have great difficulty in gaining ground against disease. At times they are humbled by the inadequacy of their minds and their instruments. Looking at themselves, their colleagues, and their patients, the chief characters also find human nature to be a formidable foe. Nevertheless, all of them persevere courageously despite their own and/or others' nagging questions about the ultimate effectiveness of medical research.

Chapter Two
Self-Image and Attitudes Toward Life and Success

Good literary portraits reveal, among other things, the subjects' most deeply held convictions about themselves, their lives, and success. To provide the best possible characterization of the doctor-researcher of fiction, this study includes an analysis of occupational effects on his or her self-image, definition of success, and overall attitude toward life. Generalizations will be made from character sketches of eleven protagonists and from information about the six others.

In the novels as a group, the doctor's involvement in medical research reveals a personal ambition which goes beyond, or in some instances replaces, the desire to serve. The protagonists are largely motivated by curiosity, a creative urge, and the need to achieve something out of the ordinary. Some of their endeavors are fueled in part by a desire for fame and/or immortality, and in some cases the prospects of financial reward, professional prestige, and improved social status are a factor. While nearly half of the main characters become involved in medical research because they feel that it provides them with the most effective means of serving humanity, they are also serving needs of their own. The rest turn to medical research primarily because it offers them personal rewards, though they do not begrudge humanity any benefit from their work. The novels show, however, that motivations can change in the course of a career or even during a single research project.

Most of the central characters' self-concepts also undergo changes. Though all the scientists necessarily have an underlying faith in their ability to succeed in the tasks they have undertaken, their confidence is sometimes shaken in the long, painstaking, and frustrating process. To varying degrees, those whose work is either upstaged or discredited feel like failures despite the successful completion of their projects. Those who have achieved success in their profession at the cost of happiness in their personal lives also feel defeated to that extent. On the brighter side, most of the chief characters discover themselves, as it were, in medical research: they have found the field in which they can excel and have taken up the work which best uses and most challenges their abilities.

In most cases this work is directly or indirectly responsible for putting the protagonist's life in perspective. Many of the main characters see medical research as a calling—their true calling. Others see it as the work of their own choosing. In any case, being in this occupation not only tends to make the doctor look at himself or herself more objectively but also brings about unexpected events which may change the context in which the doctor sees his or her life. Furthermore, involvement in medical research gives life such an intensity that for most of the central characters, life is all but meaningless without it.

One of the novels which reveals most about the introspective side of the doctor-researcher is Betina Ewerbeck's *Angela Koldewey*, which will be discussed in some detail here.[1] It has been singled out not only because it emphasizes the chief character's reflections on her life but also because it offers unique insights. Angela Koldewey, the only female protagonist who is a medical researcher,[2] has more to contend with than her male counterparts in this profession dominated by men. In addition, this young woman of the Germany between the two world wars learns that she is dying from the disease she is investigating. This knowledge causes her to hold life very dear and to become preoccupied with leaving a legacy to humanity. But all of her attitudes, those which are typical in the subgenre as well as those which are not, shed light on topics important to the present study.

Already an "achiever type" by nature, Angela Koldewey is quite conscious of being one of very few women in medicine, and therefore has an added incentive to achieve. Very early in the novel, she is asked by a male medical student why she is studying medicine. She is used to this type of question and hears in it the underlying comment, "Ich verstehe nicht, wie Sie, die Sie doch gar nicht hässlich sind, sich eine Arbeit aufbürden, die Sie gar nicht nötig haben" (8). Considering that she is in such a profession when she could easily have found a man to support her financially, Angela's colleagues either admire her courage and dedication or see her as some kind of eccentric. Her concern, however, is not with the impression she makes as a woman but with her accomplishments as a doctor. While a resident and a doctoral candidate,[3] she knows that her performance will be the sole measure of her worth, and she expects no other consideration (85).

Angela is determined to succeed as a doctor especially when, because of her career, she has given up her plans for marriage. For her there is no possibility of compromise: she must give herself completely to one or the other. Letting her fiancé Martin go is the hardest thing she has ever had to do, but sacrificing her main goal in life would have been much worse. The narrator calls Angela's feeling for her profession a passion which causes her love for Martin to die (66) and a fire inside her which makes her feel godlike and euphoric (66-67).

The author Ewerbeck highly dramatizes Angela's final decision to renounce marriage and become a doctor; the strength of Angela's determination is underscored by the physical effect of the feelings involved. As Angela cries, "Ich will Ärztin sein!" she feels as if her body has become a single blazing flame, and she trembles with overpowering emotion (44). Her self-assertive cry is like "der Schrei eines Gefangenen, der endlich das Geständnis ablegt, das ihm die Freiheit bringen soll," and after uttering it, she lies down and weeps with relief (44). The liberation brought by this "confession" is like an exorcism of Angela's pain and past illusions about life: "Aller Schmerz, der sie in den letzten Monaten täglich durchzogen hatte, brach aus ihr hervor und riss zugleich alles aus ihrem Innern fort, was sie bisher vom Leben erträumt und erhofft hatte" (44-45).

Notwithstanding Angela's determination and dramatic decision, treating severely ill patients really tests her faith in herself. This work, which she considers her specific calling, is very hard on her because she becomes so emotionally involved with her patients and cannot accept her helplessness when they die. She feels that she has been given a mission but not the strength to carry it out: "...es war, als ob gerade die Bürde, die Angela zu schwer erschien, für sie gedacht war" (40). Her work in medicine is much harder and less glorious than she imagined when she first decided on her career at the age of seventeen.

Research work, on the other hand, builds up Angela's self-confidence. For her doctoral work she is assigned to assist a professor in his investigation into the cause and cure of malignant granuloma, an always fatal but slow-working illness that seems to be on the increase.[4] The challenge of the project is particularly appealing to her as is her particular assignment, studying case histories for any similarities and doing follow-up work with patients. In this project, Angela has found her niche: "Sie spürte, hier hatte sie die Arbeit erhalten, nach der sie sich gesehnt hatte, die ihrer Kraft entsprach" (82). Before long, her doctoral assignment has become her work for life: "Das war keine Doktorarbeit mehr. Das war ein Ruf, ein Schrei, der an sie erging" (99). She is sure that her healing power and her talents have been intended for this project. On her research mission, Angela feels like an explorer pushing through unknown territory, and she is determined, confident of success:

Sie sah die Aufgabe vor sich ausgebreitet wie ein Neuland, das sie zu bereisen hatte, es war kein Sehnen mehr in ihr, wenn sie daran dachte, sondern ein fester Wille, der nicht lockerlassen wollte, ehe er sich bis zum Ende durchgerungen hatte. (91)

A colleague's inability to appreciate Angela's feeling for her work betrays a lack of faith in her ability to achieve her research goal and thereby brings the spark within her to a red-hot glow. Hans von Düren, who later becomes Angela's husband, wonders aloud why she has not chosen a less demanding doctoral project. He finds her whole orientation toward her profession unrealistic and tells her that she is reaching for the stars. She answers him confidently, "Ich werde erreichen, was ich mir vorgenommen habe" (105). Angela feels that the success of her research project—the discovery of a cure for malignant granuloma—is within her reach, however many years of hard work and self-sacrifice it may require.

Angela has definite ideas about the purpose and plan of her life. She feels that she has to achieve something for the benefit of humanity in order to justify her existence and to give her life meaning (136). She considers herself ready even to sacrifice her life in service to the sick, having declared theatrically, "...ich will ihnen in der grössten Not beistehen—Schritt um Schritt mit dem Tod um sie ringen. Und wenn es mein Leben kostet..." (44). Although sincere, she is completely unaware of the prophetic nature of the latter utterance: she does not know that she will develop a terminal illness while conducting research.[5]

Appropriately named, Angela is sure that her calling is from God: "Kam der Wunsch, ihr Leben den Kranken zu opfern, nicht auch von Gott? War diese Aufgabe ihr nicht von Ewigkeit her gestellt worden?" (106). Her calling is therefore not only an opportunity but also a very serious, almost overwhelming responsibility: "Sie sah, dass dann eine Verpflichtung auf sie gewälzt war, die eines Menschen Kraft überstieg. Der Ewigkeit verantwortlich!" (106). On the other hand, she feels a special bond developing between herself and God, eternity, the world, etc.; she is sustained and gratified by the thought of having a permanent place in the Master Plan:

Aber in dem Masse, wie sie fühlte, dass ihre Aufgabe wuchs, fühlte sie auch eine neue Verbundenheit in sich mit dem Wesen aufkommen, dass [sic] Gott, Ewigkeit, Welt, alles war. Und sie wusste, sie hatte einen unvergänglichen Halt gefunden. (106)

Unfortunately, all her positive feelings about herself, her work, and her chances of success are lost immediately when she finds out that she has contracted the very disease she has been studying. She is stunned by the discovery. She feels robbed of her plans and goals, duped, betrayed by heaven, and therefore stripped of her self-confidence and self-esteem:

Alles war von ihr abgesunken. Alle Pläne, alle Ziele. Sie war nicht mehr die Starke, Mutige, Unbesiegbare—sie war arm, verlassen, hilflos. Nichts war ihr geblieben. Sie hatte alles einem Glauben geopfert, der sinnlos war. (136)

Angela feels that she has given up the happiness of married life for a baseless belief. On the other hand, she mourns for her life's work, cut off just when it has begun. She may be able to work only three years more, which is not enough time to find a cure for malignant granuloma.

Angela despairs because the only thing that can give her life meaning is achievement—a specific, lasting accomplishment. She has the highest requirements for her personal contribution to the world: "Es soll bleiben, es soll weiter wirken, es soll reichen bis zu den letzten Menschen, bis zur Ewigkeit" (140). She cannot be content with adding in a general way to "das Gute auf der Welt" (140); therefore, spending the remainder of her life doctoring exclusively is not an option for her. She will feel like a complete and respectable human being again only when she can find a way to achieve something of perpetual significance.

At her lowest emotional point, when she feels like a walking specter, Angela has a sudden revelation: her mission in life is to give birth to a child, whom she can shape into a great achiever. (Her limited research has shown that her disease is neither contagious nor hereditary, so she sees no reason why she should not experience married life and motherhood.) She says to herself, ". . . das Kind wird die Erfüllung meines Lebens sein!" (150).

With her new plan, she regains the sense of mattering, of belonging to the world of the living. She feels like herself again, except that she has a solemn sense of purpose in place of her earlier ebullience: ". . . ein tiefer Wille, ein grosser Glaube war über sie gekommen, der sie wieder zu dem Menschen machte, der sie war, als sie ihr Leben den hohen Zielen weihte" (146). She has a renewed relationship with nature: "Sie fühlte sich verwoben mit der Natur und voll glücklicher Ruhe" (147).

As a wife and mother, Angela feels fulfilled. Once she has written up her preliminary research work and submitted it for her doctorate, she gives herself completely to marriage and to motherhood. She learns to be very happy with her husband Hans (Martin would never have done) and is delighted with her son Volker, who develops just as she has planned.

However, despite the fact that her life as a wife and mother is full and rewarding, she cannot forget her inability to achieve her original goal. And the author cannot let Angela's research work simply be abandoned. At one point, Angela suddenly remembers the great work and wonders who will carry it on: "Wie ein unbezwingbarer Berg tauchte plötzlich die Arbeit in ihr auf, die grosse Arbeit, die sie begonnen und von der sie abgelassen hatte. Wer würde sie nun zu Ende führen?" (179).

Ironically, Angela provides for the continuation of her research by becoming disabled by the disease. When the malignant granuloma has weakened her visibly, Hans decides to take over the project in the hope of saving her life. She is happy to be a catalyst in the work, but vicarious achievement is not enough for Angela Koldewey. She comes to play a more direct part in the project: though bedridden, she is able to advise her husband in the research. While Hans does the laboratory work, she mentally sifts through all the findings. Her observations and suggestions, supported by her own case history, prove invaluable. This involvement gives her a joy that compensates for the suffering from her illness and helps her fight the feeling of helplessness against the steady advance of death.

With Angela's help, Hans makes such rapid progress in the research work that Angela sees her original goal almost reached in her lifetime. She lives just long enough to hear details of the recognition given their work at the most important German medical congress. The conquest of the disease within reach, Angela dies radiantly happy that she and Hans have achieved something of lasting importance: "Ich bin so glücklich, wie ich es nie geglaubt habe. Das grosse Werk gelungen! Ich habe es noch erlebt. Es ist etwas geschaffen—was der Welt—bleibt" (230).

As this last statement indicates, success for Angela Koldewey includes more than the completion of her particular research project and more than achievement in general. Here and elsewhere in the novel, there are evidences that she is obsessed with achieving immortality. Soon after she learns of her fatal illness, Angela considers tending patients full time but asks herself, "...kann ich damit etwas von bleibendem Wert schaffen? Was mich lebendig hält, auch wenn ich gestorben bin?" (139). She later hears an inner voice saying, "Angela, du willst doch nicht nur glücklich sein um deiner selbst willen. Du willst doch glücklich sein, weil du etwas geleistet hast, weil du etwas geschaffen hast, was dich, dein Wesen auf der Welt, weiterleben lässt" (143). A great factor in her desire to have a child is the perceived need to perpetuate her influence on earth. She says, "Das Kind ist Blut von meinem Blut. Es wird werden wie ich. Ich werde nicht tot sein und von der Erde verweht— ich werde mit allem Besten, das ich habe, weiterleben" (146). And her last words to her husband show that she is determined that death shall not end her earthly presence: "Ich bleibe bei dir—mit meiner Kraft, meiner Seele, meinem Glauben" (230). Her last wish, though it may be read as purely altruistic, can be seen as a desire for another type of immortality—lasting distinction and a place in history: "Hans, denke daran, ich will—das letzte Opfer dieser Krankheit sein" (230). Perhaps the author considers a certain preoccupation with winning a place in human history to be an undeniable component in the motivation of the achiever type, even the altruist.

At any rate, Angela Koldewey finally considers her life to have been a success. As the novel ends, there is good hope that she and her husband will forever be remembered as the two who cured malignant granuloma.

Far from seeing herself as the victim of a tragedy, she says, "Gott, ich danke dir, dass sich mein Leben so erfüllt hat" (230).

Martin Arrowsmith is completely different from Koldewey in the way he sees himself, his life, and success.[6] He does not see himself as a servant of God or of his fellow human beings, and he feels no need to justify his existence. He considers his life his own to do with as he will, even if his plans are sometimes thwarted. His work becomes his whole life simply because medical science interests him so much and provides the best possible creative outlet for him. Martin comes to find that his self-expression through research is its own reward, but in the meantime he often desires other compensations such as fame and money and the things that money can buy. He does not, therefore, share Angela Koldewey's obsession with achieving immortality; he is more concerned with what he can actively enjoy in this life.

Since a much longer period of time is covered in *Arrowsmith* than in *Angela Koldewey*, the greater character development is seen in Martin. In his career in medical science, he progresses from the conceit of a young zealot to the humility of a more mature scientist and finally to the cautious self-confidence of a seasoned professional. He also changes from a seeker of fame, fortune, and adventure to a contented workman.

The process of becoming the great researcher he hopes to be is a very humbling and often discouraging one for Martin—all the more so because of his initial pride. When newly acquainted with the language and method of science, he feels generally superior to his fellow medical students, who are not very interested in scientific medicine. In fact, he hopes to be recognized as a genius. But although Martin does have the best scientific mind in his class in medical school, his study in bacteriology makes him—for the time being—"curiously humble" as he discovers the remarkable extent of his ignorance (41-42). Later, when Martin temporarily throws over science in favor of medical practice, he feels relieved of the "intolerable strain of learning day by day how much he did not know" (109). Yet after having made this choice, he makes many false starts in his career and sometimes feels like a failure. Then, after he has returned to science and become a full-time researcher, he no sooner starts to feel comfortable with himself than he is made aware of great deficiencies in his scientific education. In his laboratory work he has many frustrations on the way to important results. And unfortunately, what the public and the popular press take for Martin's great triumph is, as already mentioned, actually a scientific embarrassment to him. This failure, however, results in a more consistent and determined allegiance to science, which helps Martin maintain a certain degree of objectivity with regard to himself. From that time on, his honesty and his personal standards do not let him remain satisfied with his achievements for very long. Only quite late in the novel, after much harder effort than he ever could have imagined, can Martin afford to be pleased with the level of his knowledge and his work.

But objectivity aside, it is largely Martin's abiding (if sometimes battered) belief in himself which enables him to attain excellence in research. His second wife, Joyce, pays a tribute to his faith in his abilities when she asks him, "...are you going to admit there's anything you can't conquer?" (393).

Martin's thoughts about just what he should do with those abilities go through many changes, as do his ideas about his image and his role in medicine. Unlike Koldewey, who feels secure in a friendly medical community, Martin is restless and dissatisfied as a student and as a doctor. At first, he sees himself in the role of the noble reformer who is going to bring scientific methodology to medicine and somehow drive out the laggards and money grubbers in the profession. But when he sees the extent of the opposition to reform, he begins to feel more like a renegade than a crusader. Progressing as a medical scientist, he becomes increasingly proud of being a renegade—except when the need for employment and then enchantment with success soften his tone for a while. At the end of the novel, Martin and his partner Terry have become monastics of science, purists living and working in the wilderness; but upon leaving civilization, Martin reveals that he prefers to think of Terry and himself as pioneers (425).

Whereas early in his career, Martin enjoys being called "lie-hunter" and "truth-seeker" by his wife Leora, he later comes to believe that a person may find many truths but not one final Truth. He says that Truth is "a skeptical attitude toward life" (260). Having reached this conclusion, he temporarily stops yearning for recognition as a genius or a guiding light: "He insisted that no one could expect more than, by stubbornness or luck, to have the kind of work he enjoyed and an ability to become better acquainted with the facts of that work than the average job-holder" (260-261).

All that Martin finally wants out of life is the freedom and the means to do the work he most enjoys; however, before he comes to this realization, his expectations are not always so humble. From time to time, he thinks about receiving worldwide scientific acclaim and all that goes with it—a position of authority, more money, better social standing, and the mention of his discovery in textbooks. He dreams of world travel and the good life. But when actually at work, he has no place in his mind for thoughts of personal glory and great prosperity: "...when he was back at his bench the grandiose aspirations faded and he was the sniffing, snuffling beagle, the impersonal worker" (300-301). Learning to define success is Martin's main accomplishment in his maturing process.

This ongoing lesson is not without cost; pursuing unworthy goals takes more away from his scientific endeavors than do his research failures. Martin gets sidetracked at each phase of his career, seeming to need to experiment with false notions of success in order to convince himself that they are not for him. As a country doctor he finds out that small-town routine and respectability are not substitutes for professional fulfillment. In a large midwestern town, he discovers that getting in with the smart set does not satisfy him for long. At a clinic for the rich in Chicago, where he is much overpaid by sleek, prestigious, and not particularly scrupulous surgeons to do routine laboratory work, Martin soon feels that he has sacrificed self-respect and his very idea of life because he has laid his best skills aside. While with a large and famous research institute in New York, he is seduced by professional prestige and learns "the horror of the shrieking bawdy thing called Success, with its demand that he give up quiet work and parade forth to be pawed by every blind devotee and mud-spattered by every blind enemy" (309). For a time he is lulled by the comfortable life of the rich elite, and he even experiences family life. These benefits, however, come with strings attached. The resulting entanglements keep him from what he really desires, completely unencumbered research work.

In order to set his own course and his own terms, Martin finally walks away from everything that is usually considered essential to success. He needs to be more than "a machine for digestion and propogation and obedience" (425). Leaving his wife and child, he says, "We could prove that I'm a hero or a fool or a deserter or anything you like, but the fact is I've suddenly seen I must go! I want my freedom to work" (425). The only permanent state which Martin Arrowsmith would finally call success is that of being allowed to try to achieve his potential.

The hero of A. J. Cronin's *Shannon's Way*, though very independent-minded like Martin Arrowsmith, finds recognition for achievement so important that he cannot feel successful without it.[7] At the completion of his all-consuming research project, Robert Shannon feels that his faith in himself is confirmed and that his insistence on following his own way has been justified. But when he finds out that someone else has just published the same scientific findings, his tremendous research effort becomes meaningless to him. He considers himself a self-made failure. His own solitary, stubborn way, "that tortuously winding path," has led him back to where he started (304).

Through most of the novel, Shannon's self-image as a medical scientist is much like Martin Arrowsmith's.[8] Shannon, like Arrowsmith the novice, sees himself as a seeker of truth (60). He, too, sees himself as a renegade and an irrepressible scientific investigator. He so believes in himself and in the importance of his own scientific work that he refuses to waste his time collaborating with his supervising professor, even to keep the very advantageous Eldon Fellowship. He cannot abandon his way and ignore his "inner compulsion" and his "inspiration" without selling himself, he says (60). But he realizes the larger consequences of his independence: he must "take issue with authority and fate" (18). Shannon's world, like Arrowsmith's, is much more hostile than Angela Koldewey's: while she is one with the world, Shannon considers himself "alone, one against the world" (25).

He also shares Arrowsmith's early aspirations to fame: "I was young,...burning with the painful ambition of a silent and retiring nature, longing, in my poverty and obscurity, to astound the world" (20). Arrowsmith, however, is shown maturing beyond this point whereas Shannon is last seen only a few weeks after his thwarted attempt to gain international recognition. The reader is left with the feeling that Shannon's great desire has not been altered by his great disappointment.

Like Koldewey and Arrowsmith and others, Shannon cannot be content with doctoring. When his attempt to make a career of research appears to have failed, family pressure threatens to force him into general practice in and around his little home town. He knows that his heart will never be in such work: "I should grind along, without interest, blunting the edges of my ambition, mediocre, indifferent, and defeated" (306-307).

For Shannon as for Koldewey and Arrowsmith, feeling successful is tied to being able to use all the best that he has; however, in Cronin's novel it seems that a good position in research is a prerequisite for success, and a widely recognized achievement is the ultimate goal. As things turn out, Shannon receives an offer to lecture in bacteriology at a Swiss university, where he will also be able to make a promising new start in his own research. He will no longer have to take confining, undesirable jobs in order to have the use of adequate laboratory facilities. His chief supporter, Jean Law, predicts that despite his "terrible reverse," Shannon will go on to do "finer, greater work" (310).

In *Shannon's Way*, as in many other novels, the main character requires something else in order to feel successful: the love and companionship of the right person of the opposite sex. Success and failure in love have a very marked effect on the hero's self-image, and the help and moral support of Jean Law are very important to his research itself. At the end of the novel, after Shannon realizes that he has won the love of this woman who was nearly lost to him forever, he has "no thought of failure" (313).

Georg Letham's self-concept and general outlook on life and success are affected profoundly by his participation in one very special medical research project.[9] His preoccupation with his own experiments having brought out the worst in him, Letham is led by a series of events to become part of a team researching yellow fever. This work and certain indirect benefits from it give his life purpose and elicit new positive responses. A larger context is thereby provided for his ideas about his personal significance.

While Letham's private research work does not change his personality or, by itself, make him become a criminal, it does intensify certain undesirable character traits—his coldness, his antisocial behavior, his lack of respect for anything but knowledge and wealth, and his lack of concern for anyone's needs but his own. He indicates that his playing a godlike role with regard to his laboratory animals makes it somehow natural for him to deal with his wife in the same manner (24). When Letham sees the opportunity to free himself from his wife's smothering love and to finance his experiments with money from her life insurance, he coolly gives her the lethal injection mentioned earlier.

The protagonist and narrator acknowledges the apparent incongruity of his being a scientist and a criminal, a doctor and a murderer (9); but he makes no excuses for what he has become. He simply points out the connection between "das Verbrecherische" in the realm of morality and "das Pathologische" in natural science (7). Given this association, it is somehow fitting that this man capable of cold-blooded murder should be fascinated by deadly diseases.

Letham's crime confirms all the worst that he has noted in his character—the traits mentioned above—and underscores his helplessness to change. In the introduction of this intricate psychological study, Letham says that he is always alone in the deepest sense, incapable of faith in anything (8). Although he claims a great love of beauty, completeness, and perfection (9), he also sees himself getting no better and no wiser as he grows older (8). After he has been sentenced to life in a penal colony for killing his wife, Letham is certain that his existence will always be "das überflüssigste Ding auf dieser überflüssigen Welt" (245).

He has cynical words for life in general and for his own life in particular. He often mentions the senselessness of existence. He says that what he saw as a military doctor-researcher in World War I has convinced him of the worthlessness of the life of the individual (27). The individual, he believes, is powerless to change anything (8). Letham feels that only through riches and knowledge can one gain a somewhat firm footing in life (8); therefore, his goal is "Möglichst viel zu wissen und möglichst viel zu besitzen" (11). At one time he calls money the surest foundation in the present world order (11). But despite his comfortable fortune, he seldom feels that happiness in life is attainable for him: "Glück hatte ich, aber glücklich war ich selten" (12).

Letham will certainly accept any rewards that his scientific efforts may earn him, but he has no delusions about any ultimate feeling of success through research. He suggests that positive results of an experiment do not give meaning to life or change anything in the long run; they do not bring happiness or peace or lasting satisfaction because the researcher turns immediately to a new problem as soon as the present one is solved (27).

Unlike Angela Koldewey, Georg Letham does not have the advantage of believing that his life is ordered and directed by God. His life, in fact, has only the appearance of being directed toward a goal at all; although he lives for his experiments, even they give him no real satisfaction:

Meine Laufbahn schien nur von aussen zielbewusst und gradlinig strebend—in Wahrheit war sie es nicht. Hätte ich denn sonst in und von Experimenten gelebt? Ausserhalb des Experiments hatte ich keinen Genuss, ja überhaupt keine Verbindung mit dem Leben. Aber *im* Experiment? Habe ich wenigstens hier Befriedigung gefunden? Ich muss sagen, nein. (24)

In this frame of mind or an even worse one because of his exile to a penal colony, Georg Letham comes to the big research project of his career; but this work alters his life and his outlook considerably. Instead of being forced to do hard labor, he is assigned to the penal colony's quarantined hospital to help two other German doctors find out how the yellow fever virus is transmitted. He notes a change in himself at his first view of death caused by this dreadful disease (245). This new research work gives him a positive purpose and a much better general attitude: "...ich hatte ein wahrhaft durchdringendes Gefühl der positiven Notwendigkeit meiner Existenz und—der Notwendigkeit der Existenz auch der anderen" (247).

Indirectly, the yellow fever project causes another change in Letham's life. He falls in love with a beautiful young Portuguese girl who is dying of the disease. Although any personal relationship with this girl is doubly doomed from the start, Letham's proven ability to love does a great deal for his perspective and his self-image. He says, "Mein Leben ist ein anderes geworden" (269).

However, it is Letham's love for his work which makes the biggest difference in him. His meaning and identity as a person become inseparable from his great task, and in this he is like Koldewey except that he neither feels called by God to this endeavor nor concerns himself with making a lasting contribution to the world. Motivated instead by personal gratification from the research and by his fascination with this particular intellectual challenge, Letham toils doggedly under miserable conditions. Volunteering himself as a test case to prove that mosquitos spread yellow fever, he nearly dies of the disease. Such is his personal stake in proving his theory. He says, "Ich war dabei. Ich blieb dabei: diese Spur war die Mühe wert. Es war meine Sache, es war *mein Krieg,*...meine Aufgabe" (316).

When he and the other remaining team member finally obtain the proof they have been seeking, Letham does not glory in the success; rather, he experiences a great emotional decline. He says that earlier in his life, such an accomplishment in research would have made him proud and vain; he would have accepted any and all honors and awards as his due, as partial compensation for his efforts (496). But things have changed for him: "Ganz anders jetzt und hier. Mein persönliches Leben bedeutete mir nichts mehr, wenn ich keine Aufgabe hatte, die es in Form einer derartigen Arbeit ausfüllen konnte" (496). Considering his great task complete and knowing that he will never again have such important work to do, he feels that his existence will once again seem worthless, superfluous, and meaningless (496).

As it happens, however, Letham must taste defeat before he can mourn his victory; and instead of losing his sense of purpose in life, he loses his faith in himself and what he has accomplished. When the local medical authorities arbitrarily reject his and his partner Carolus' findings, Letham starts to doubt his theory, himself, and everything. Rather than question the authorities' judgment, he says with self-deprecation, "Ich war an meiner Gottähnlichkeit irre geworden" (500).

Luckily for Letham, he and Carolus not only obtain permission to prove their theory in practice but also have years more of important work to do. They lead the effort to protect the populace of the island from the disease-carrying mosquitos and systematically exterminate these insects. Letham wins his "war," eventually helping to eradicate yellow fever in an area larger than Europe.

After this goal of the massive undertaking has been reached, Letham fades from the scene; he even ceases to have an identity. His name does not appear anywhere in his group's published report, and he reveals at the end of the novel that he has not even been using his real name in the narrative (502). His story closes with the words "Ich verschwand in der Menge, und das ist gut so" (503).

Nevertheless, Letham, as he must be called, has left behind something permanent that can be traced to him—his story. The writing of it has been, as he says in his introduction, an experiment, an attempt to elucidate all that he has experienced (8-9). He has wanted primarily to observe himself with "wissenschaftlich prüfendem Blick" as in a mirror (9), but his compulsion to document his life may also be related to Angela Koldewey's desire to become immortal by means of a legacy.

An especially significant research project also leads Josef Zeppichmann to change his ideas about his life and his own importance.[10] Initially a thoroughgoing egoist who bolsters his sense of worth with his hope for success in medical research, he comes to value humanity's possible benefit from his project even more than his own life.

At the outset, young Zeppichmann is extremely self-centered. Coming from a poor, backward, stifling community, Josef wants to demonstrate what a self-made man of science and medicine can do with his life. More than any of the other protagonists, he is motivated by the promise of social respectability and professional prominence. If need be, he will risk years of "poverty, overwork, loneliness" (99) for the success of his research (and for the recognition it should earn him); but the thought of becoming "a plain, good doctor" is "frightening" to him (99). Giving himself completely to medical practice would not only make him feel stagnant, but it would also considerably reduce his chances of making a name for himself.

Besides, Josef tells himself that in research he has found a high purpose in life. He has developed a drug that kills tubercle bacilli and, with a few modifications, will be completely safe to inject into human beings. His research may one day make one of the worst scourges of humanity a thing of the past. In the meantime, seeing the recovery of tuberculous guinea pigs he has treated, Josef has "felt his first great happiness" and a sense of triumph (65).

He is aware, however, that "triumph cannot be enjoyed in privacy" (66). He already has the details planned for achieving international acclaim. Anticipating this reward, he is "whipped by a scarcely tolerable impatience" (66).

Generally pushy and occasionally cocky, Josef shows signs of a great and only partially fulfilled need for ego support. The narrative suggests that Josef's sometimes abrasive manner is the result of overcompensation for his feeling that people look down on him, a poor, unattractive, small-town Jew in post-World War I Germany. At the same time, his research work has given him a feeling of professional expertise and personal significance—much the same effect that Angela Koldewey's project has on her. The difference is that Josef is concerned not with his calling but with his showing. He is even perfectly willing to sacrifice a tubercular patient's life in order to advance his own project and thereby increase his chances for professional success.

However, during the only human experiment which Josef conducts, something happens which starts a complete change in his priorities. He falls in love with his subject, a sickly, unrefined, poorly educated maid named Minna. Discovering how much he values her and then experiencing at the hands of the Nazis how it feels to be considered usable but expendable, Josef realizes the evil of making any person the means to one's own ends. Having become a terminal tubercular himself by the end of the novel, he sees his life as unimportant compared to the goal of saving Minna and, through that process, saving countless thousands of others.

Ignaz Philipp Semmelweis, the central character of both *The Cry and the Covenant* and *Semmelweis, der Retter der Mütter*, also comes to see himself and his life as unimportant compared to the work he has begun with his research.[11] The collective cry of all the women suffering with childbed fever seems to be an appeal to him personally, and he feels called by God to find the cure for the disease. Toward the end of *The Cry and the Covenant*, he swears, "I'm going to save women.... As long as I live I'll do with what I must. And I'll never stop" (371). But he adds humbly, "I never mattered" (371). Sober reflections and his work with patients correct some inflated notions of himself that he has held for a short time. He says, "I'd gotten to believe that I was...the source of remedy—even the remedy itself. I'm just a middleman.... I'm not the road. I'm a guide" (*Covenant* 380).

Semmelweis' great humility is also due to his unique experience as a medical scientist. His research leads him to the cause of childbed fever and also to a horrible truth about himself: his own hands, contaminated with material from the diseased cadavers which he has been examining by the hundreds, have been spreading death. The irony of this situation is bitter. In *Covenant* Semmelweis' recognition of his guilt is "painful and depressing" (239). In *Retter* the narrator says, "Mörder! klang es ihm in die Ohren" (31). However, solving the mystery of the murder and learning how to stop the spread of the disease more than compensate for his responsibility in so many deaths.

Walter Töpfer's involvement in research, by bringing a higher purpose to his life, gives his self-image a big boost; but the cost of succeeding in this new work appears to be more than he is willing to pay.[12] As a full-time family practitioner, Töpfer laments his powerlessness to cure many of his patients and his inadequacy to meet their various needs. When he also complains that no one has yet developed an antitoxin to help him combat tuberculosis, his wife Eva challenges him to produce it himself. She shows him how they two can manage their finances so that he can give up his practice in order to live and work in a sanitorium and devote himself to research. Though Töpfer at first has no confidence in his ability to succeed at a task which has already proven too difficult for many great minds, he demonstrates in the course of his project a rare skill that has gone undiscovered and unused for too long. Unfortunately, the Töpfers' temporary separation, essential to Walter's scientific work, threatens to become permanent. Once aware of this real danger, he starts to lose his taste for professional success.

Not far into his research, Töpfer becomes convinced that his project is a great work, and it becomes his whole life. The narrator says, "Die Arbeit frass ihn vollständig" (70). Although Töpfer makes some false starts, his dedication and talent confirm Eva's faith, "dass in ihm was Besonderes steckt" (14). He who once thought it an effrontery to imagine that he could succeed where so many great researchers had failed (30-31) even begins to speculate about winning the Nobel Prize (57).

Making a contribution to medical science does not, unfortunately, guarantee overall happiness in life. After Eva decides that Walter has no room in his life for anything but research, she asks for a divorce. When Walter finally realizes what has been happening to his marriage, he questions his recent notion of success. Thinking that he has thrown away everything he had with Eva, he asks himself if triumphs in the laboratory are really more important than having such a wonderful woman (176). He weighs the worth of all of Eva's youthful charms against "die Anerkennung von ein paar alten Professoren" (176). Though he achieves most of what success in his profession is supposed to be—publication of an important article about his work, recognition and praise, and even appointment to a prestigious research institute—it seems a hollow victory to him.

Töpfer's marriage is saved, however, and he discovers, or rediscovers, that his definition of a successful life emphasizes things other than fruitful medical research and humanitarian accomplishments. There is no happiness for him without Eva and a secure home life. He has also come to realize how much he would like to have a son. Though not, like Angela Koldewey, obsessed with achieving immortality through progeny, he has thought how fitting it would be to have a son to continue building what he leaves unfinished (152). And at the end of the novel, while admiring his baby boy, Töpfer betrays some sentiments much like those of Koldewey after all: "...dieses Kind war Walter Töpfers Sohn. Sein Fortsetzer. Der Grössere nach ihm, der vollenden sollte, was er mit saurer Mühe begonnen hatte. Der seinem Blut Ewigkeit schenkte, seinem Samen Unsterblichkeit" (231).

There are, of course, accomplished professionals who live without lasting companionship or the prospect of offspring, and such a one is Alex Addams.[13] Although Addams passionately loves research, enjoys worldwide respect and acclaim for his various scientific undertakings, and has a secure position in a large, prestigious institute in a big city, he is not fulfilled in his personal life. Early in the novel, the childless Addamses agree to a separation because in their many years of marriage, they have not been able to give each other what they need. Although

Alex Addams' professional life has always seemed "abundantly and pressingly purposeful" (91) and has borne fruit, his private life is one of "forever seeking communion" (5).

Therefore, Addams must qualify any evaluation of himself. When he reflects on a newspaper's descriptions of him as "eminent biophysicist" and "Logical nominee for the Nobel" (4), he knows that no such praise is due Alex Addams the private person. Considering his marriage, he feels "exasperation at his failure in these years to find the peaceful fulfillment of his spirit's aspiration" (4). Addams' estimation of himself as a medical scientist is in sharp contrast with his self-image as a companion: in the laboratory he consoles himself with the thought, "Here I have failed no one" (15).

Although Hans Lennhoff also fails in marriage while succeeding in research, he is perhaps somewhat less to be pitied than Addams.[14] At the end of the novel, the narrator says that the hero, whole-heartedly enjoying a rest between the accomplishment of one important mission and the undertaking of the next task, has come to know the best experience that life has to offer. Lennhoff has learned to accept the life style dictated by his profession and to deal with both success in his work and failure in his private sphere.

When he tries to make room in his life for marriage, Lennhoff is not aware that, as the narrator states several times, the select few researchers who have been destined to make major breakthroughs are not allowed the luxuries of a spouse and friends. It is perhaps more cruel than kind that Lennhoff is allowed to experience warmth and companionship at all: his marriage is short-lived, having created a conflict impossible to resolve. While he enjoys the company of his wife Renate, he is also obsessed with finding the cause and cure of a new deadly disease called Palang-Negah fever. This research work, frustrating and unpromising though it is, has become his very life. Therefore, the woman to whom he has pledged himself sees so little of him that she feels married in name only. Renate tolerates this situation for about a year.

As for Lennhoff, his thoughts about himself, his work, and life in general are also brought into conflict by the marriage. On the one hand, he thinks himself a fool for spending almost all of his waking hours in the laboratory while his "entzückende Frau" waits for him at home (127). And when he makes a point of spending time with Renate and going places with her, he begins to appreciate how much of the good life he has been denying himself: "Herrje, schliesslich hab' ich doch ein Recht zu leben wie jeder andere auch!" (127). He asks himself if he has been chasing a phantom in the laboratory while forgetting "das Leben, das blühend und bereit, ihm Freude zu schenken, neben ihm einherging" (128). On the other hand, he cannot let his research work alone for long without feeling that he has been shirking his duty. Lennhoff does not know how or why he has been called to find a cure for Palang-Negah fever, but he knows that he must complete this research task he has taken on. After two weeks of rather forced attention to his marriage and to recreation, he is impatient to get back to unrestricted work. He has had more than enough of "dieses Leben 'wie jeder andere auch'" (134).

Lennhoff is, after all, a totally dedicated and unassuming professional. When he achieves the first part of his research goal, isolating and identifying the Palang-Negah microbe, he guards against letting success go to his head. When he finds himself enjoying the recognition of his colleagues and feeling as though he has been admitted to the sacred inner circle of science (234), he cautions himself against becoming vain: "Sei nicht so eitel, alter Junge. Von einem Behring oder Pasteur bist du noch weit entfernt" (227). However, as he presents his report to a large medical congress, he thinks not about himself but about the disease he must yet conquer (237). His is "der hochmutfreie Stolz" of a person whose achievement has cost great effort (236-237).

Success is not a permanent state of being for Hans Lennhoff; he does not allow himself to be satisfied with what he has accomplished, nor does he confuse the rewards with the goal. He turns down an offer to head a department at a new research institute because he has not yet accomplished his mission. He feels that he must go to the Malaysian province of Palang-Negah to join in mortal combat with the epidemic. And if he defeats this disease, there will surely be a new *Aufgabe* for him somewhere else.

While there is no lasting feeling of success for people like Lennhoff, the narrator suggests that they do briefly experience the best that life has to offer: "Vielleicht war es das Schönste überhaupt, was dieses Leben bot: im Selbstbewusstsein der gelösten Aufgabe, der nächsten schon entgegengehend, unbeschwert die kurze Pause zwischen beiden zu geniessen" (257).

As Henry Baker learns in *Medical Meeting* by Mildred Walker, life may also offer a researcher the greatest disappointment—having success snatched away before it can be enjoyed.[15] Baker, aided by his wife Liz, works for twelve years developing a new tuberculostat, only to have his discovery eclipsed by someone else's better new drug of the same type. As a result, Baker's self-image and his whole career as a researcher are brought into question.

At a big medical meeting where he is to report on the fruits of his and his wife's long, hard labor, Henry Baker is stunned when a research collective discloses better results in the same specific area. Baker's own medical breakthrough, of which he has been so proud, now seems meaningless. He feels that his belief in himself has been misguided and that the twelve years of hard work and self-denial have been in vain. He feels especially sorry that Liz has sacrificed so much for his sake; and so, for a time, does she. Since their project has had positive results, Henry cannot call himself a failure; instead, he feels like something perhaps worse—a mediocrity. Having thought that he might be one of the rare persons who find "something new or important enough to mark an advance" (106), he now considers himself just one of the many dreamers who let other people down. His belief that he and Liz, with their simple laboratory facilities, "could have discovered something as effective as penicillin, that they could name it, as you name a child, and give it to the world" now seems "preposterously childish" (106).

Henry's reaction to the unforeseen turn of events at the medical meeting reveals that his purposes in research have not all been so noble as he and others supposed. Most people, including Henry himself, have wrongly assumed that he has been driven to find a cure for tuberculosis simply by the desire to eradicate the disease that killed his mother. Before his big disappointment at the medical meeting, Henry assures himself that fame has never been the "spur" for him (68); later, however, he cannot be so certain. Liz believes that he was not sincere when he said, "If I thought someone else could do it better [research a cure for tuberculosis], and would do it, I'd give them my findings" (138). She feels that it has always been very important to him to be the one to make the discovery. She thinks that he has, in fact, counted on success (138). And Henry himself, though he once doubted his ability to do something that Robert Koch could not (26), must admit that he probably has "mixed himself up with a myth and thought he was another Louis" (140).[16] Henry's former roommate, now a psychiatrist, thinks that Henry, humble as he is, has also had ambitions (110). The latter has certainly considered the possibility of winning praise, recognition, and prestige in his profession, not to mention better pay and the chance to devote himself to research without having to earn a living at doctoring.

After the medical meeting, Henry renounces any ambitions in research; his desire now—or so he thinks—is to have a steady, well-paying private practice or clinical job so as to provide Liz with financial security and a better life than he has been able to offer her in the last twelve years. He comes very close to accepting an administrative position that would allow him no time in the laboratory.

However, he realizes just in time that any such choice would require him to surrender his identity. Research is his life. Therefore, at the end of the novel, he decides to accept a temporary situation that will pay him a modest salary to test his drug's effectiveness in combination with other medications.

The author clearly indicates that Henry should in no way be pitied. Indeed, Henry's final decision to stay in research is the triumph of his great spirit. It is the supposed good fortune of his friends and colleagues which is lamentable. Permanent mediocrity in a job that requires mostly administrative and public relations skills is the prize of the man to whom Henry is assistant. Henry's buddies from medical school days are far more ambitious; in fact, they have been so busy getting ahead that they have lost sight of their dreams of doing pioneer work in medicine. Though they have comfort, wealth, and social standing, they will never experience the pride of creative scientific accomplishment or the intensity with which Henry lives.

The case of Henry Baker shows that ego rewards are a strong motivating factor for even a humble and basically altruistic researcher. All of the other central characters as well are driven by the need to achieve something important, by the thrill of discovery, and by the great desire to succeed at a sustained creative endeavor. Even the very business-like and service-oriented Robert Koch knows the "Rausch der Entdecker-freude."[17] The possibility of recognition by the medical science community, if not by the general public also, crosses the minds of all the main characters.

As already seen, however, the strength of their desire for the applause of others varies; and fame, once attained, may lose its savor. Robert Koch, for one, cares little for popular acclaim although he is quite pleased with two of the many honors he receives. At first he remains untouched by the "Überschwang der Begeisterung" and wants to be nothing more than "ein echter Demokrat im Staatsgebilde der Wissenschaft" (264). Later, Koch, like Alex Addams, experiences how fame can widen the gap between personal happiness and professional success: "Je populärer der Name des grossen Forschers in der Welt wird,...um so einsamer wird der Mann selbst, um so anspruchsloser und verschlossener" (299).

Other protagonists sometimes see prosperity and elevated social status as the goal of their work, but in the final analysis, they do not consider these rewards as important as the success of their projects. Besides, all of them know that the probability of "making it big" in research is not great. To be sure, Martin Arrowsmith (among others) demonstrates that a medical scientist who is credited with making a discovery or a new application deemed very significant may gain fame, wealth, improved social standing, and a position of professional authority;[18] but the cases of Henry Baker, Nikolas Persenthein, Ignaz Philipp Semmelweis, and Robert Shannon show that researchers whose discoveries are not regarded as the first or the greatest of their kind may not be compensated for their efforts at all.[19]

Many of the chief characters do stand to reap large financial benefits from their research, but profit is by no means the strongest motive for them. Alfried Kalsten in *Patrouille gegen den Tod* is far more interested in the final outcome of his team's African research mission than in the small fortune which a mining company has paid him for his dangerous work. He says philosophically, "Man kann auch mit Weisskohl und Hammel glücklich werden."[20] Martin Bertram in *Viele sind berufen* hopes to have his injectable anesthetic mass-produced and marketed worldwide, but being the one to develop it means more to him than getting rich. Besides, his earnings will be used to establish a research institute. In *The Undaunted* Richard Cameron and a chemist friend develop a liver extract which is then produced commercially in pill form and distributed widely for the treatment of pernicious anemia. Cameron's share of the profits from the product is never mentioned, and he seems not to care about any earnings of this type. His concern is that his patients and others with the same disease be able to receive the life-saving substance without having to eat liver every day. William T.G. Morton in *Narkose*, on the other hand, obviously thinks about his potential earnings when he takes out a patent on his device to administer ether; but the original and strongest intent behind his research has always been to help humanity conquer pain. In *Die japanische Pest* Fritz Wieser, a slaving *Kassenarzt* in economically depressed Germany, accepts a lucrative one-year research position with the Japanese government in order to improve his family's life style.[21] However, were he not fascinated by bacteriology in the first place and led by premonition to investigate a developing Oriental threat to the whole world, Wieser would never take such a job.

Curiosity and the creative urge can provide very strong motivation, as mentioned previously. Richard Cameron epitomizes the researcher who is motivated almost exclusively by the desire to explore and to do something creative and useful with what he or she discovers. Cameron is neither mesmerized by the prospects of fame and fortune nor "consecrated to the pursuit of truth" (157). Speaking for medical researchers in general, he says, "...we are just human beings who want to find out things instead of making money" and denies any motive "much higher or much lower than curiosity" (157).

He shrugs off the fame that comes after his successful treatment for pernicious anemia causes a great stir in the world of medical science. Admittedly, Cameron, who is "devoid of pretended modesty," finds the attention "very pleasant" (236) and would enjoy seeing the effect of his sudden prominence on certain people he dislikes (277). Nevertheless, he does not allow his status as "acclaimed discoverer of a cure for a hitherto uniformly fatal disease" to go to his head (237). He knows that the colleagues who congratulate him are not admiring him but the work he has done (237). Besides, he knows that many other researchers were very close to making the same discovery (237).

As indicated above, Cameron is not interested in becoming rich. For one thing, he has very simple tastes and cannot even imagine what he would do with "surplus money" (276). For another thing, he is very scrupulous. He flatly refuses a twenty-thousand-dollar bonus and a soft job offered him in exchange for his endorsement and promotion of a poorly made version of his diet supplement. He calls the offer a "bribe" to do "dirty work" (301). And morality aside, money is not nearly as important to him as job satisfaction. At the end of the novel, he sacrifices financial security rather than lose the chance to do some exciting new research work.

For the same reason, Cameron is not ambitious for a position of prestige and authority, either. When offered the directorship of the newly created Pernicious Anemia Foundation, he turns it down because he wants to stay active in the laboratory. The only real regret he has about rejecting the administrative position is that he is keeping the financial future very uncertain for his wife Judith. Were only he concerned, the choice would be easy:

To be back in a laboratory, at a microscope, peering at blood smears,...edging every day a little farther into the unknown—how could he turn away from that to sit in an office and write letters and talk to salesmen and tell men in search of work that there was nothing available? (307)

Cameron also finds that he has no taste for relaxation and the so-called finer things of life, the prizes many people work so hard to earn. Once he has completed the part of anemia research that most interests him, he takes Judith to films, concerts, and all kinds of stage productions. He also has time to read literary and philosophical works. He gets little pleasure from any of these activities, however. Having time to "enjoy life" makes Cameron very restless and unhappy: "For six years he had thought, talked, breathed, pernicious anemia and now he was tormented by the emptiness of life without an absorbing central endeavor" (290).

Judging from the illustrations above, one can say that a medical scientist's career has several general effects on his or her basic self-concept and ideas about life and success. The activity of medical research, it seems, discloses truths about the researcher as well as the matter under investigation. Both kinds of truths aid in the doctor-scientist's maturing process in his or her professional and personal life. Not all changes in attitude are necessarily for the better, of course, but the great majority of the long-term ones are positive. Obviously, medical research work provides a niche and a new and higher purpose in life for all the protagonists. While they differ in their beliefs about the source of their calling to their profession and the nature of their responsibility for the use of their time on earth, they tend to value life—theirs and others'—more highly because of their work. Most of them find, however, that their profession does not allow them a very well-rounded sort of existence. On the other hand, to the overwhelming majority, life without research work holds little of lasting interest. In this work, the main characters discover their highest potential. Consequently, they form a more objective picture of themselves and their importance in the larger scheme of things. They may consider the larger scheme of things to be the progress of humanity, the Master Plan, the course of nature, the advancement of science, or simply their personal exploration of the unknown; but in any case, they all learn to subordinate transitory gratifications to this greater cause.

Any central character's definition of success, however, reflects his or her greatest personal needs as well as this conception of the greater good. As one might expect, all of the researchers are driven by selfish as well as altruistic concerns, which differ among individuals and change as those persons mature. Many of the medical scientists are at times strongly attracted by the prospects of the money and/or prestige which their research may eventually bring them. Achieving immortality is a daydream or latent desire of a few of the chief characters, and it becomes a downright obsession for one, Angela Koldewey. Sheer curiosity, the need for meaningful work and a creative outlet, the need to excel, and the wish to accomplish something for science or humanity are the motivations in most of the novels. In the final analysis, success, while it presupposes at least adequate pay and equipment, is not dependent upon the rewards which society bestows on celebrities. To the protagonists it means worthwhile achievement and the freedom to continue developing toward their potential. Nevertheless, credibility and some recognition for accomplishment are undeniably important to them. As for success in life overall, the novels show that the researcher, like everyone else, needs communion. Every one of the main characters indicates the need for a partner—a spouse in most cases—with whom to share life.

Chapter Three
Physical and Mental Health

The authors of medical research novels are unavoidably concerned with their protagonists' occupationally related physical and emotional problems. The health of these medical scientists is threatened on every side; some threats are very minor but persistent while others are quite serious. Although there are portrayals of robust, tireless medical researchers who almost never lose a day's work due to illness or exhaustion or worn nerves, the physical or mental health of the great majority of the main characters is sooner or later adversely affected by their profession. Even at best, research can be stressful and very tiring. At worst, it can jeopardize the scientist's mental stability and even his or her life.

Health risks are depicted not only because of the authors' desire to present realistic detail; they also serve to heighten the drama of the narratives and add the element of irony. Nine of the chief characters, in the course of their research work, knowingly risk their lives.[1] Even less severe occupational health hazards serve as obstacles which bring out the central characters' courage and determination. Irony is created by the fact that the medical researchers, who more than anyone else should be conscious of the need to maintain a healthful regimen, either cannot or will not take proper care of themselves.

Appropriately, there is a recurring metaphorical link between sickness or madness and the researcher's drive to create or achieve. For example, in *Helfer der Menschheit* Robert Koch's "Drang zum Schaffen" falls upon him like a sickness.[2] The narrator of *Semmelweis, der Retter der Mütter* says of his hero's zeal to carry out his mission, "Wie Fieber, wie Krankheit war es über ihn gekommen."[3] In *Viele sind berufen* Martin Bertram himself senses that his "Wut des Schaffens" is "eine Art Krankheit."[4] When Martin Arrowsmith is asked if he is "perhaps a little insane," he replies, "Oh, absolutely! And how I enjoy it!"[5] W.B. Erlin's narrator in *Die Spur* says that Hans Lennhoff is possessed by the demon of the disease he is trying to conquer.[6] Nikolas Persenthein in *Zwischenfall in Lohwinckel* exhibits a "Besessenheit von der Medizin, die ihn alles in Fetzen reissen liess, was nicht in seine Richtung passte."[7]

For most of the protagonists, medical research is not a safe, sane occupation. But as indicated in the first chapter of this study, a special type of personality is required for this work; and the main characters have a professional passion which overcomes their instinct of self-preservation.

A very good novel to illustrate how a medical researcher's mental and physical health can be affected by the profession is *Viele sind berufen*. Martin Bertram, in his dedication and persistence—and consequently, in his virtual disregard for his own health—is typical of protagonists of medical research novels.

As a staff doctor in a hospital, Martin takes his health for granted after he becomes obsessed with the idea of developing an injectable general anesthetic. He lives like a monk in the laboratory, devoting all his off-duty waking hours to chemical experiments. He pushes himself to exertions that are both "übermenschlich" and "unmenschlich" (113). The least serious problems caused by his laboratory work and his preoccupation with it are flat feet, headaches, and mental "absences" during conversations. Trying to ignore the fact that the strain is doing him harm, he continues to overexert himself. Consequently, his physical and emotional problems increase in seriousness. His drive to create allows him little sleep, and the great amount of tea he drinks to keep awake at work causes him to lose his appetite. Overworked, unrested, undernourished, and overstimulated by caffeine, he exhibits symptoms of abnormal nervousness; occasionally his brain just shuts down, as it were:

Er schläft kaum mehr, ungezählte Tassen Tee haben ihm den Appetit verdorben, ganz abgesehen von gewissen nervösen Symptomen, mit denen er sich auch noch herumbalgen muss. Manchmal kann er einfach nicht weiter. Kurzschluss. Das Gehirn gibt nichts mehr her. Aber das geht gottlob immer wieder vorüber. (63)

Martin does not keep up such an insane pace for the entire three years of his research project, but late in the novel, his health is seriously threatened by overwork, stress, lack of rest, and malnutrition. In a non-paid position at a research institute, Martin depletes his savings before he completes his project. He cannot buy enough to eat, and because of his constant worry that someone will beat him to his research goal, he dares not take time off from his work for sufficient rest. Therefore, his resistance to disease is very low. After a day or two of not feeling well, he is beset by an "entsetzliche Angst" that he will become seriously ill; in his run-down condition, a case of the flu could keep him confined to bed for a long time (423).

During the most stressful periods of his experimentation, Martin's nervous condition is deplorable. He experiences irritability, extreme jumpiness, despondency, apathy, susceptibility to fearsome dreams and imaginings, paranoia, and self-destructive impulses. At his lowest point, he is so exhausted physically and emotionally that he is beyond caring about what happens to him: "Wo ist seine Abwehrkraft hin? Sein Behauptungswille? Er möchte sich fallen lassen ins Bodenlose" (147).

Although Martin rebounds from this state, he is sometimes fearful of the ultimate effects of all of the physical and emotional stress, especially after his closest friend cracks under strain. In fact, this worry itself becomes a stress factor. Martin knows that the success of his research project depends on the strength of his nerves:

Das Ganze ist jetzt eine Nervenfrage. Manchmal ist mir, als taugte ich überhaupt nicht mehr zu ruhiger, methodischer, disziplinierter Forschung, alles Krampf und Zuckung. Ich fahre zusammen, wenn im Institut ein Instrument zu Boden fällt... (432)

In all fairness, it must be mentioned that Martin's worst nervous states are not entirely due to the particular stresses of his research work. He is working as a doctor without a license and greatly fears being exposed and ruined. So great is his anxiety that he even considers murdering a patient who knows about his past. However, he actually worries more about not being able to finish his project than about losing his career as a physician.

Paradoxically, when Martin decides to test his general anesthetic on himself, he does not seem upset about the possibility of dying. Without any dramatics, he instructs his assistant to inject him with the "Narkophen" and note what happens. In addition to its predicted effect, the drug gives Martin's heart a shock that a weakened heart might not have withstood. Nevertheless, Martin considers the risk of his life just part of his job:

Vielleicht hätte er sogar das Recht, sich als Märtyrer der Wissenschaft zu fühlen. Aber so fühlt er nicht, keine Rede davon. Wenn ihm was passiert—Betriebsunfall. Kein Grund, sich etwas darauf einzubilden. Jedem Beruf sein Risiko. (130)

Many of Martin Bertram's counterparts in other novels are also willing to risk their lives for the sake of their research. As mentioned earlier in this study, Georg Letham, to help prove his theory, allows himself to be bitten by a mosquito carrying the yellow fever virus and as a result almost dies of the disease.[8] At the end of *The Fire and the Wood*, Josef Zeppichmann allows his tuberculin, which has proven very nearly fatal to his one human experimental subject, to be tested on himself and no one else.[9] Martin Arrowsmith, testing his bacteriophage in the plague epidemic, is well aware of the possibility that he himself could succumb to the disease. Robert Koch risks fatal illness on various research missions to sites of epidemics. Despite his seemingly unassailable health, repeated and prolonged stays in the tropics (combined with his normally sedentary lifestyle) result in premature hardening of the arteries and irreversible weakening of the heart.[10] Semmelweis in *The Cry and the*

Covenant intentionally causes his own death to further his scientific cause.[11] After he has exhausted every other means of making the world understand how childbed fever is spread, he puts his cut hand into a putrefying cadaver, insuring that he will die of the disease he has tried to conquer.

The dangers of Morton's research in *Narkose* also merit mention here.[12] Hoping to produce a general anesthetic that can be inhaled, Morton administers various gases to himself. In the course of his experimentation, he hallucinates, suffers severe nausea, and sustains serious damage to his lungs. When he tries ether on himself, he is not certain whether he will ever awaken from the induced sleep.

Researcher Alfried Kalsten and his assistant Maxie Perussenko in *Patrouille gegen den Tod* find a unique and perilous solution to a research problem.[13] Having no other available means of transporting live specimens of a virulent microorganism to their laboratory thousands of miles away, they inject themselves with the germs. Thus, to conclude their already risky research mission in Africa—one which has subjected them to the dangers of heat prostration, poisonous insects and snakes, other harmful wild animals, unfriendly natives, and various tropical diseases—they willingly become carriers of an as yet incurable and always fatal illness.

Fritz Wieser in *Die japanische Pest* is the ultimate representation of pathologists who constantly live with the danger of death from infection.[14] He conducts tests on a microbe which multiplies so rapidly that it can kill a human being within thirty minutes after exposure. When Wieser accidently nicks his finger on a slide teeming with the deadly microbes, he immediately and unflinchingly cuts off the finger to keep the germs from spreading to the rest of his body. His coolness while doing so fills his onlooking colleague with awe.

Notwithstanding the cases cited above, most of the occupational health risks which confront main characters are not major, though they are perennial. For example, the adverse effect of laboratory chemicals on human hands is mentioned in *The Cry and the Covenant, Semmelweis, der Retter der Mütter, Helfer der Menschheit,* and *Medical Meeting*.[15] Blurred vision and other symptoms of eye fatigue bother Hans Lennhoff and Robert Koch because of the amount of time they spend using a microscope. Koch's ribs ache from long hours of pressing against the edge of the microscope table. Researchers' chronic shortage of sleep due to their work is practically a cliché of medical research novels. Additionally, several of the central characters have difficulty in sleeping when they do make time for it. Martin Arrowsmith, Hans Lennhoff, Georg Letham, and Robert Shannon experience short-term insomnia.[16] The combination of insufficient sleep, overwork, and stress produces recurring headaches for Shannon, Josef Zeppichmann, and Nikolas Persenthein. Lennhoff, Arrowsmith, and Bertram experience dizziness when they have driven themselves too hard.[17]

Almost all of the chief characters overwork themselves, and most of them generally take good health for granted.[18] At times of intense research activity, some eat improperly or very irregularly and most try to ignore their need for rest, diversion, and physical exercise. Though they are doctors, they seldom concern themselves about the long-term effects of such habits.

Robert Koch, with his negative attitude toward taking good care of his health, is the classic example (and perhaps the prototype) of the driven researcher. Koch considers such things as meals, relaxation, and sleep to be bothersome interruptions to his work: "Essen, Schlafen, Erholung waren die überflüssigsten Dinge, die jemals erfunden worden waren. Keine Unterbrechung konnte kurz genug sein" (211). His ability to keep up a hectic pace is seemingly due to sheer force of will and, of course, a robust constitution. Although he becomes overweight due to his sedentary life style and prematurely gray, Koch is until the age of 62 almost always in fine working form and "mit Vitalität derartig geladen, dass er jeden Augenblick explodieren könnte" (217). At times, however, he is also ready to explode in the sense of being nervous and irritable. But like Martin Bertram, Koch realizes the importance of steady nerves in his work and so on rare occasions gives in to his need for prolonged deep sleep.

Richard Cameron is neither as rugged nor as lucky as Koch and therefore does not get away with neglecting his health.[19] Refusing to stay in bed for two or three days when he has two seemingly minor health problems, he ends up losing much more time from his work. "Feeling illogically that to refuse acknowledgment of illness might somehow stave off collapse" (218-219), he does nothing about a persistent cold and an infection in his ankle. When he subsequently has to be hospitalized with a severe case of influenza, he is "toxic as the devil and crazy as a coot" (223). A friend and fellow doctor tells him, "When it comes to your own health you haven't got any more sense than a bum on the streets" (224). Not until later in the novel, after he has had a foot amputated, does Cameron start taking good care of himself and exercising conscientiously every day.

Nikolas Persenthein is a prime example of a doctor-researcher who not only neglects his health but also abuses it. He sleeps hardly at all but keeps himself going with exactly those items of diet that he disapproves for his patients: "Alles, was er für tief ungesund und verderblich hielt, brauchte er selber in grossen Mengen" (14). For example, he consumes much heavily spiced fried meat and strong coffee and smokes a great many cigarettes. On especially strenuous days, Persenthein wants a glass of wine with his meal. To keep himself feeling fit, he takes cola tablets and a tonic containing strychnine. For his frequent headaches he takes Veronal (barbital). Only once in the novel is he unable to work when he wants to, but he is always tired and irritable, old for his thirty-eight years.

Like Persenthein, many of the other main characters rely on chemical substances to compensate for the irregularities of their regimen and the hardships of their profession. Several depend heavily on tobacco and caffeine to keep them awake and alert.[20] William T.G. Morton and Martin Arrowsmith both have a problem with alcohol abuse. And in the latter part of his life, Morton inhales ether to soothe himself when he is especially upset. Morton's use of ether as means of escape is, in fact, responsible for his death: in a heavy ether-induced sleep, he falls off a park bench, rolls into a river, and drowns.

In every case, the substance abuse is a reaction to job-related tensions. Looking at particularly troublesome aspects of the work of Persenthein and Morton and Arrowsmith, one can see various sources of stress besides the obvious ones of overwork and time pressures. Anxieties and setbacks of many kinds beset these medical scientists, who receive insufficient moral support and appreciation when they need them most. The other main characters have most of these problems as well but for various reasons react differently.

Persenthein's greatest irritants are the lack of resources for proper experimentation, the lack of support for his theory, and the continual uncooperativeness of the one human subject in his research. As mentioned elsewhere, Persenthein sees himself at odds with established medical science because of his radical idea, which also helps create friction between him and most of the townspeople of Lohwinckel. Barely making a living and trapped in the small, backward town, Persenthein cannot test his idea on the scale it deserves. And although Lungaus, his experimental subject, originally agrees to the strict regimen which Persenthein has prescribed for him, he repeatedly contaminates the doctor's experiment by eating or drinking what is not allowed.

Although Arrowsmith's terrific emotional strain during the testing of his new vaccine in the horrible plague epidemic has already been mentioned, the stress factors bear reiteration here. The nightmarish atmosphere in which he must work, the heavy moral responsibility for his insistence on vaccinating only half of the local population, the animosity of and pressure from the other half, the threat of death due to the plague or to desperate islanders, and the loss of his wife and a very close colleague combine to bring about an emotional breakdown and send Arrowsmith on a long drinking binge.

Compared to other fictional medical researchers, Morton has little pressure or conflict during his project; but afterward he is unbearably frustrated by his former employer's success in stealing much of the glory and reward for his discovery. Furthermore, he is incensed by humanity's failure to show proper appreciation of his contribution to medicine. As indicated by problems with drug abuse, Morton does not cope well with his feelings of outrage and loss.

The central characters' tensions, physical and mental fatigue, and complete preoccupation with their particular projects are responsible for other problems besides substance abuse. These factors cause anything from absent-mindedness to a complete inability to function normally in society. As might be expected, overwork, added to the normal difficulties of research, makes almost all of the chief characters jumpy and irritable at times. Continual discouragement gives rise to temporary apathy in some cases. The narrowness of focus in protagonists' lives and their relative isolation during their projects tend to produce in them an emotional imbalance and to alienate them from the mainstream of humanity and even from their loved ones. The combination of emotional stress, mental strain, and loss of perspective due to lack of outside interests, added to physical exhaustion, can cause neuroses; and the main characters whose strain or frustration is too great become psychotic.

Absent-mindedness, though a commonplace hazard of virtually every profession, deserves special mention in the case of Robert Koch, who shows how bad mental absences can become for a medical scientist. On the way home from work one day, Koch is so engrossed in thoughts of his research that he walks past his house. Only after some time of wandering aimlessly does he remember where he wanted to go.

A good picture of the irascibility of the fatigued and discouraged researcher can be seen in *Die Spur*. After Hans Lennhoff has tried unsuccessfully for two years to catch sight of the microbe responsible for Palang-Negah fever, he comes close to the emotional breaking point. His laughter, a hitherto rare phenomenon, sounds like "das Lachen eines Menschen, der nahe daran ist, die Herrschaft über sich zu verlieren" (21). Lennhoff is sometimes so disheartened that he feels like scrapping the whole project. More often, he feels like snarling at his laboratory assistant, who sometimes growls back. Then the two revile each other like "Berserker" and swear like "Lastträger" (90). The exchanges of abuse are a healthy thing, however, allowing Lennhoff and his assistant to vent their frustrations and preserve their sanity:

Erbittert, entmutigt, voll ohnmächtigen Zorns, hilflos gegen die durch nichts zu bezwingenden Widerstände. Bis endlich einer als erster das befreiende Wort fand. Dann lachten sie. Dann verspotteten sie sich selbst. Dann schimpften sie sich ihre Verbitterung aus dem Leibe. Und danach ging's wieder eine Weile. (90-91)

Apathy, a reaction of many of the researchers at some time, is seen by Georg Letham as a natural consequence of extensive research without results. He calls apathy a kind of intellectual paralysis or state of despair:

Wenn...eine wissenschaftliche Untersuchung über eine gewisse Zeit angedauert hat, ohne auch nur die geringsten positiven Resultate ergeben zu haben, ergreift den Forscher eine Art Lähmung, eine intellektuelle Verzweiflung, eine sture Apathie. (294)

A more persistent emotional problem for many of the central characters is that of alienation, which is especially well illustrated in *Zwischenfall in Lohwinckel*. Nikolas Persenthein is so obsessed with his revolutionary medical theory and his long-term experiment that his mental and emotional contact with the other important things in his life—his wife, his child, and his medical practice—is seldom what it should be. Although his experiment does not require him to be physically isolated in a laboratory, he is quite alone in the realm of his thoughts most of the time. Being the only doctor in a very small town, he does not have even one colleague at hand with whom he can discuss his theory. Persenthein's great new idea makes him change and lose touch with the rest of the world: "Sie machte ihn fremd, alt, voll Kanten und Beulen, sie stellte ihn mitten in ein Vakuum, einen luftleeren, unmenschlichen Einsamkeitsraum, diese Idee, die er hatte oder die ihn hatte" (14).

Alex Addams, seeing the alienation of the researcher as a given of the profession, has a very philosophical approach to the subject. The scientist, he says, "can speak intelligibly [about his or her work] only to other scientists, to those who know his language and have lived in this peculiar state of mind"; and he adds, "It is this that cuts him off, makes him almost an alien among men" (81).

A far worse condition develops for two of the chief characters who press on toward their research goals despite severe mental, emotional, and physical fatigue. Martin Arrowsmith and Robert Shannon show what can happen when the researcher refuses to slacken a dangerous pace.

Arrowsmith develops a classic case of nervous debility. What may make even more of an impression on the reader than the symptoms of Martin's condition—extreme irritability and sick nervousness, impairment of physical coordination, serious absent-mindedness, obsessive behavior (including the compulsion to spell words backwards), paranoia, and various phobias—is Martin's detachment in observing himself:

As sharply and quite as impersonally as he would have watched the crawling illness of an infected guinea pig, Martin watched himself, in the madness of overwork, drift toward neurasthenia. With considerable interest he looked up the symptoms of neurasthenia, saw one after another of them twitch at him, and casually took the risk. (303)

Fortunately, taking the risk causes Arrowsmith to lose only about a week of quality work. He is able to function completely normally after he goes on a hiking and camping expedition in the wilds.

Not so the shattered protagonist of *Shannon's Way*. Robert Shannon's nervous breakdown, of which an account is given in the second chapter of this study, is cured only after several weeks of complete rest. Shannon's condition before his breakdown is marked by symptoms very much like Arrowsmith's but is also aggravated by painful personal losses. Shannon has a self-destructive bent as well, or perhaps his outbreak of rage is directed against his perceived failure rather than against himself. In any case, Shannon's attack of nerves is climaxed by his destruction of the flasks of vaccine which he has produced at the cost of so much hard work and sacrifice. He is stopped just before he sets fire to his research notes, and then he loses consciousness.

Two other main characters actually lose their sanity because of their research projects. Semmelweis and Morton are driven mad by disillusionment and frustration with established medical science and rage over the injustices done them after their years of hard work and privation.

As discussed elsewhere, what Semmelweis has to do to demonstrate the truth of his doctrine of antisepsis is almost maddening in itself; but he also has to endure his colleagues' scorn and ridicule while battling their shameful indifference to overwhelming scientific proof and to the possibility of saving millions of lives. After exhausting every effort to make the world heed his message, Semmelweis dies a broken man in an insane asylum.

Morton is emotionally undone by his earlier-addressed troubles in winning proper recognition, appreciation, and other rewards for introducing the use of ether as a general anesthetic. His former employer, Dr. Charles Jackson, persists in claiming priority in the discovery and succeeds, temporarily, in turning public sentiment against the use of ether. While other individuals are able to capitalize on Morton's medical advance, Morton himself is not, to any great degree.[21] By the time Morton does start to receive official recognition and prize money for his discovery, he has become a drunkard and a maniac who raves about taking back his great gift from an unworthy humanity. Although he lives quietly and fairly normally toward the very end of his life, he never fully regains sanity.

The medical research profession, as presented in the novels examined here, can be a hazardous one both physically and mentally. More than half of the central characters literally risk their lives, and the overwhelming majority eventually develop one or more physical or emotional problems that are connected with their work. These problems evidence not only the protagonists' insufficient attention to their own well-being but also the intricate connection between the body and the mind. The novels also illustrate the principle that everything—even seemingly selfless endeavor to increase medical knowledge—must be compensated in some way. All of the highly motivated researchers overcome much and give up much; but those who cannot or will not take time for proper nourishment, rest, exercise, and some diversion pay for it eventually. And some of the researchers whose dearly bought achievements are not recognized or appreciated develop very serious problems.

Chapter Four
Close Relationships With Other People

In general, the protagonist's relationships with other people are no less important in the medical research novel than in any other type of novel. The main character's emotional involvements reveal much about him or her as a person. In the novels discussed here, the medical scientists' successes and failures in relationships also say much about the benefits and demands of their chosen work. Like many other types of professionals, these researchers experience the dilemma of needing companionship but not feeling able to devote enough time and attention to friends, lovers, and relatives. For this particular type of professional, there are also special factors which inhibit close relationships: scientific training, the scientific mindset, and certain personality traits typical of people who are attracted to medical research work.

As a rule, the fictional medical scientist, very achievement-oriented, is not gregarious by nature. In many cases, he or she finds that other people make for unwanted distractions from work. On the other hand, some of the central characters are not easily enough distracted—that is, they are so enthusiastic for their work that they take little notice of other people or their own need for them until it has become very difficult to remedy the situation.

A few of the chief characters have an even more serious handicap in relationships: being conditioned to lay emotions aside in professional life, they also tend to suppress emotions in private life and therefore seem inaccessible to other people. To compound this problem, many of them either consciously or subconsciously regard their work, and especially the laboratory itself, as a haven from the uncertainties, irritations, and pain which punctuate intimate affiliations of individuals. The researcher with this attitude may not only seem but also become inaccessible to fellow human beings. Besides, in another way, he or she is truly unreachable—at least to people not in the profession. That is, the vast majority of outsiders have no proper understanding or appreciation of what the medical scientist is doing at work. And since any dedicated professional's work is virtually his or her life, this type of gulf in communications has serious personal implications. All of these factors as well as various individual ones work against the development and maintenance of lasting bonds with other people.[1]

In general, therefore, the central characters maintain very few intimate relationships. While all of them have at least one serious romantic involvement, more than half end up with no really close friend of their own sex.[2] Although all but three protagonists are married at some time, few maintain a healthy marriage and a satisfying home life for long. The main characters' relationships with family members also tend to be adversely affected by their work. Contact with parents or siblings, if the latter exist, is rarely shown. Siblings or children of protagonists are significant characters in very few of the novels, and only one of the researchers is really a good parent.

The effects of medical research on the chief characters' personal lives are not all negative, however. Typically, work brings the doctor-scientist in contact with at least one person who provides moral support, relief from the stresses of research, and communion of some sort. For more than a third of the central characters, a colleague of the same sex becomes a good friend. In most of the novels, an important relationship develops between the protagonist and a close associate of the opposite sex. Predictably, most of these attachments produce romantic interests as well.

In the following discussion, the most important personal relationships are considered as belonging to either home life or the work environment. As a matter of convenience, all relationships with family members are grouped together, regardless of the actual residence of any given relative. For each of the two categories of relationships, pertinent details from one novel in particular will be examined, but references will be made to several other novels as well.

Die Spur, W.B. Erlin's paean to the modern medical scientist, illustrates especially well the effects of an exceptionally dedicated medical researcher's career on his home life.[3] In this novel, Hans Lennhoff's long, intense investigation into the cause of a newly discovered deadly disease so consumes him that there is very little of him left for his wife Renate. Although Lennhoff, aged 39, truly loves his 33-year-old bride, he finds that he cannot make any compromises which affect his research work. Renate, on the other hand, will not make compromises with regard to her ideal of marriage. They are divorced about a year after their wedding.

For some of Lennhoff's colleagues, however, a lasting and satisfactory marriage is possible. The novel shows the dynamics of one of these successful partnerships while identifying the causes of the Lennhoffs' marital failure.

Erlin's obtrusive narrator suggests in various ways that Lennhoff, despite his feelings for Renate, should not have married. It is obvious that, except on rare occasions, Lennhoff has no time for or active interest in anything but his work. Though the narrator emphasizes the wife's rather than the hero's shortcomings, the reader can see that Lennhoff really has almost nothing to give to marriage. Lennhoff does, however, have a destiny to fulfill, and that takes precedence over everything else.

For two years before being introduced to Renate at his superior's home, Lennhoff has been completely submerged in the international effort to find a cure for Palang-Negah fever. Despite spending twelve to sixteen hours a day in his laboratory, he has been unsuccessful in even identifying the microorganism which causes the disease. Almost all the rest of his waking time has been taken up with reading professional journals, corresponding with colleagues in his specialized field, and brooding over his research problems.

Although Renate makes Lennhoff aware that life offers more than work, he is almost always too preoccupied with his laboratory procedures to think about anything else—despite the genuine thrill he feels in this young woman's presence. He breaks a date whenever he feels that an experiment cannot be interrupted. He does, to be sure, take a few days off for their wedding and short honeymoon; and for a two-week period later in their marriage, he conscientiously dedicates time to Renate. Nevertheless, Lennhoff does not basically change his working habits just because he has taken a wife. Indeed, sometimes he comes home only to sleep.

Ironically, Renate is first drawn to Lennhoff because of his earnestness and his zeal for his work. He is impressed by her because she seems serious and quiet and capable of vision. These two lonely souls fall in love because each feels so appreciated by the other. Life for each of them seems to be making a new beginning. Unfortunately, it is not; they find that they have very little in common.

Lennhoff does not share Renate's interests. Soon after their wedding, she is moved to ask him, "Was kann ich mit meinen schwachen Kräften weiteres tun, um dich aus deinem Laboratorium wegzulocken?" (70). He reads professional journals on their honeymoon trip, and at their destination, he visits medical supply stores, a medical bookstore, and a research institute. After the fourth day of their honeymoon, he yearns for his laboratory and has no more feeling for the amusements of the big city. His attitude being what it is, Renate gives up on the idea of a vacation. Then at home, after he has resumed his work with renewed enthusiasm, Lennhoff seems to stop noticing his wife's or their home's appearance. He very rarely takes Renate anywhere, and he does not want the distraction of visitors when he is at home. He encourages Renate to have company and to undertake things on her own, but socializing means nothing to her without him. Lennhoff has no time for social life and tells Renate that he does not know what to say to people: "Weisst du, ich hab' so schrecklich viel zu tun und kann wirklich keinen einzigen Gedanken für Konversation aufbringen!" (99). Conversation with Lennhoff also becomes increasingly difficult for Renate because of his one-track mind. He is "besessen von einem einzigen Gedanken: dasjenige zu finden, dem er auf der Spur war" (10).

He does not, however, remain totally unaware of Renate's lot; he is just very slow in observing the problem in their relationship. Though not frequent enough, his thoughts of his wife are tender, and he feels guilty about leaving her alone so much of the time. He acknowledges his neglect: "Ich hab' dich scheusslich vernachlässigt" (127); and later, he realizes that she has been deeply disappointed in marriage.

However, his occasional recognition of her feelings and attention to her are not enough to keep their marriage alive, especially after he resumes his old work habits. Most of the time, Lennhoff is so caught up in the challenge of his research that he simply forgets everything else.

Renate has no such ambitious and all-absorbing project other than her marriage itself; and seldom having a husband with whom to do things, she is constantly reminded of all the pleasures of life which she is denied. Alone at home so much of the time, she feels like a prisoner.

She resents and comes to hate Lennhoff's work. This hatred is only increased when she finds out from a friend that Lennhoff has been given a female laboratory assistant. Although her husband's relationship with his assistant is strictly professional, Renate is deeply hurt to think that this other woman is part of his world while she herself is not.

Despite the author's good faith in showing Renate's point of view, he virtually dismisses the fact that Lennhoff contributes so little besides good intentions to their home life. Indeed, the narrator says that Renate is to blame for the deterioration of the relationship because she has never taken an active interest in her husband's noble work. She has failed to understand, says the narrator, that Lennhoff could not be other than he is; and she has not appreciated her good fortune in having such a man:

Sie begriff nicht, dass er gar nicht anders sein konnte, dass ihr das seltene Glück zuteil geworden war, einen der echten Forscher zum Manne zu bekommen.... Und sie sah nicht ein, dass sie ja nur innerlich teilzunehmen brauchte an seiner Arbeit, um ihn bis ins Letzte zu verstehen. Sie war es, die etwas schuldig blieb, nicht er. (164)

Lennhoff is faulted—conditionally—for one thing only, his failure to perceive soon enough the growing problem in his marriage: "Wenn überhaupt, war dies sein Anteil an Schuld, dass er, eingesponnen in seiner Gedankenwelt, nicht bemerkte, dass sich die Wolke um seine Ehe immer drohender zusammenzog" (165).

From the narrator's sexist and *Forschung über alles* perspective, the priorities in the matter are clear. It is bad for Renate to have her hopes and dreams shattered, but it would be worse for her man to be prevented from doing the work that he feels called to do: "Es ist schlimm für eine Frau, ihre Träume und Hoffnungen in sich begraben zu müssen. Schlimmer noch hat es der Mann, dem nie vergönnt ist, die Arbeit zu tun, zu der er sich berufen fühlt" (43).

Lennhoff's destiny and the importance of his special mission are mentioned repeatedly. The narrator indicates that the sadness of the Lennhoff marriage could have been avoided if both parties had seen this destiny realistically from the very beginning. Early in the novel, the narrator explains that because of the hero's high calling, he has no time for friends or a wife (23). Just before the divorce, Lennhoff himself realizes that he never should have married; it has not been possible either to give Renate the happiness she deserves or to do his work wholeheartedly. Inwardly, he rebels against his fate: he spends hours in "wütender Auflehnung gegen ein Geschick, das ihm das einzige Glück, welches er ausser seiner Arbeit kannte, nach flüchtiger Dauer wieder nahm" (196).

The narrator also makes observations about the fate of the wife of any especially devoted researcher. He hints that even during courtship, Renate has, or should have, a good idea of what life with Lennhoff will be like: "Ahnte Renate, wie oft sie dieses: 'Nur heute nicht...' noch würde hören müssen?...Spürte sie bereits die Einsamkeit der zahllosen verwarteten Stunden, den Verzicht?" (53). It is indicated that had Renate occupied herself with reality instead of vague dreams and hopes, (43, 209), she would have considered the lonely and frustrating lot of the wives of the few "genuine" researchers—"einen Mann zu haben, ohne ihn doch zu besitzen, weil es für ihn nur e i n e Besessenheit gibt, die durch seine Aufgabe" (50).

The author allows Renate to have the last word about the relationship primarily so that she can confess—unconvincingly—her original error and ultimate responsibility for the rift. But at the same time, she can testify to the scientist's essential loneliness and inability to provide emotional warmth:

Jetzt weiss ich, dass wir im Grunde niemals zueinander passten, weil Hans zu jenen Männern gehört, die im tiefsten Innern immer einsam bleiben. Ich brauche aber Wärme und den g a n z e n Menschen. Vielleicht [wäre es gegangen], wenn ich mich rechtzeitig um seine Arbeit bemüht und so den Weg gefunden hätte, Aber das habe ich versäumt... (251)

Even while showing that Lennhoff should have known better than to marry, the narrator sympathizes with his hero completely. He tells of Lennhoff's great longing for Renate, which must be suppressed when she is no longer talking to him. The researcher suffers "qualvolle Augenblicke schmerzlich wild aufflackernder Zärtlichkeit," and only by throwing himself into his work can he alleviate his pain (196).

The narrator's sympathy for Renate, on the other hand, seems to have been spent long before the breakup. She has become cold, unreasonable, and unapproachable by the time her husband really concerns himself about their relationship. Her grievance is summed up and dismissed as follows: "Sie fühlte sich enttäuscht, aber sie vermochte nicht zu sehen, dass die Ursache dieser Enttäuschung in ihr selber lag" (164).

The author does not stop at having his narrator directly tell the reader what is wrong with the Lennhoffs' marriage; he also offers a portrait of what it might have been like, had the hero not been chosen for his special task and had his wife been a different kind of woman. Professor Scherrlein, the director of the research institute where Lennhoff works, has continued to have a tender, mutually fulfilling relationship with his wife Vera despite the demands of his administrative job and his own research project. The Scherrleins discuss Institute matters (including the Lennhoffs' problems) as well as their own private affairs, and each values the other's opinions. Little gestures of endearment punctuate their conversations. Analyzing the success of their marriage, Vera says, "Wir haben uns eben beide Mühe gegeben," to which her husband replies, "Mir hat es niemals Mühe bedeutet, dich zu lieben, Vera!" (210). Prof. Scherrlein obviously appreciates and meets his wife's needs, and she understands the demands of his work. Even though he sometimes spends too much time away from her and then brings his job's problems home with him, she is glad that his work is so worthwhile and so fulfilling to him. She would have no use for another type of man, she says: "Männer, denen ihre Arbeit nicht mehr bedeutet als nur Gelderwerb—ich kann mir nicht helfen—andere mögen sich damit begnügen" (101).

Of course, Vera Scherrlein is not married to a man of Lennhoff's destiny or a man who leaves her so very much alone. Her husband, a respectable but not a specially gifted researcher, confesses to Lennhoff, "Aber weisst du, das Letzte, die allerletzte blinde Besessenheit, die hat mir doch gefehlt" (103). In other words, he can offer much more to Vera than Lennhoff can offer to Renate. Scherrlein's work allows him to be home to do such things as take tea with his wife and help her entertain guests relatively often. Therefore, the Scherrleins' very healthy marriage, though it is intended to be an object lesson, cannot be used as a yardstick to measure the marriage of a Hans Lennhoff.

In showing a great researcher's natural difficulty with the most demanding of all personal relationships, Erlin has historical and literary precedent. *Helfer der Menschheit* shows a similar if more complicated picture of the medical scientist's home life.[4]

Because Robert and Emmy Koch have been married some time before he takes up microbiology, and because medical research as a field is then barely even a concept, Emmy has no advance knowledge of her husband's true calling or of the fate of great researchers' wives. A practical, capable, and industrious homemaker from a middle-class background, she does not understand his compulsion to experiment. She does know that when Koch has established a good, respectable family practice in a small town, he has reached her professional goal for him. But he is not satisfied and not mindful enough of the business end of his practice. When he is not seeing patients, he always wants to examine something under the microscope or experiment with something. On such pursuits he spends time and money recklessly, to Emmy's thinking. It is probably necessary for her to be an "eigenwillige und herrische Frau" (99): she must keep their financial affairs in order and make sure that her husband's patients pay him. Emmy sees Koch's creative impulses in the laboratory as unhealthy, just like the wanderlust which she thought she cured at the outset of their marriage. His experimentation does indeed become detrimental to Emmy: the deeper his involvement with research becomes, the less time he has for her. Like Lennhoff, Koch seems to inhabit a world that his wife cannot enter, a world of war against disease. The narrator summarizes Koch's interests thus: "Für ihn existierte nur das eine: der Feind, den er suchte" (211). At the low point of the marriage, Emmy is pictured sitting alone in the figuratively empty house which her husband uses as only a place to sleep.

After Koch has been recognized for his research work and is given a position at the Hygienic Institute in Berlin, Emmy tries to be a model wife and win back his love, but it is too late. Koch distrusts her new attitude and has no time for her, anyway. When Emmy sees that her efforts are futile, she grants him the divorce he wants. Though Koch continues to support her financially, the rest of her life is lonely and bitter.

For all his sympathy with the unhappy woman, the narrator is more interested in what he sees as the higher purposes of the man. Indeed, in expressing the importance of male destiny, he and the narrator of *Die Spur* are hardly distinguishable from one another. The former suggests, "Vielleicht mochte es immer so sein, dass der Mann als der Schaffende sich von der Romantik der Liebe löste, um wichtigere Aufgaben zu erfüllen" (210). Just as intrusively as Erlin's narrator, he states emphatically, "Schöpferische Menschen sollten sich an Frauen nicht binden!" (307). He explains that creative men live "viel zu tief im Banne ihrer Träume und Visionen" and are "viel zu sehr...der höchsten Bestimmung verpflichtet, sich selbst zu erfüllen" (307).

In this group of novels, it is rare for a dedicated medical scientist to have a lasting healthy home life. Of the sixteen marriages, four end in divorce and one in murder, largely because of the protagonists' commitment to medical research.[5] In two other cases, the doctor-researchers are so out of touch with everything but their work that they come very close to losing their wives.[6] In still another case, the main character and his wife become legally separated by mutual agreement and remain so.[7] Five obviously strong couples are parted by death, which in four of the cases is attributable to the medical research profession.[8] And two chief characters and their wives, though apparently quite happily married, have not been together long enough to prove the durability of their union.[9]

The greatest danger to the married couples' relationships is emotional strain, the most common causes of which are easy to identify. Many of the researchers' spouses are too often left alone or taken for granted or both. Even when the doctor-scientists are at home, they are sometimes no more available to their partners than when they are away at work. From the other point of view, most of the central characters are not fortunate enough to have marriage partners who are really interested in medical research or who can appreciate what it means to the person whose life's work it is.[10] But then again, much of what the spouses require for contentment and fulfillment is just not important to the protagonists.

Martin Arrowsmith's second marriage shows all of the above factors in operation.[11] For all Joyce's—Martin's second wife's—intelligence, attractiveness, wealth, and skill in the social graces, she does not understand him as well as they both initially think she does. Unlike his first wife, Leora, Joyce cannot comprehend that research work is his life. She thinks that by providing Martin with social respectability, all conceivable comforts, a laboratory at home, and a child, she has given him everything he could want. However, she has not. Martin has long since lost his interest in Joyce's social circle. Furthermore, he finds himself unable to work without being interrupted and feeling accountable to Joyce for the time he spends away from her. When he realizes that he can no longer deny his need to be entirely free for his research work, he leaves Joyce and their young son. At the very end of the novel, Joyce is planning to divorce him and remarry.

The situation is reversed in Vicki Baum's *Zwischenfall in Lohwinckel*; that is, the failure to observe and understand is all the researcher's. Nikolas Persenthein, a small-town family doctor preoccupied with testing his revolutionary medical theory, shamefully neglects his wife Elisabeth. He takes her for granted as a helpmate and rarely thinks of her as a wife anymore. He never thinks about how much his medical practice and his ongoing experiment depend on the burdensome cleaning, washing, cooking, and other daily services which Elisabeth provides in addition to her chores as a housewife. He has ceased to really see her and to communicate anything except business or routine household matters.

When Elisabeth is gone for most of one day and night, all but ready to run away with a wealthy stranger in town, Persenthein notices little except the inconvenience her absence causes him. Besides, he just then becomes demoralized by news of another doctor's similar experiment which completely dwarfs his own. When Elisabeth comes home just before dawn, she finds that her husband's despondency and inability to sleep have nothing to do with her. Apparently more concerned with his *Idee* than with his marriage, he tells her that the worst thing possible has happened to him: he has been preempted in research (279-281). Even then, Elisabeth is not insensitive to his pain: "Sie war der einzige Mensch auf der Welt, der ungefähr verstand, welchen Zusammenbruch diese Worte umschrieben" (281). By contrast, in his incredulous reply to her announcement of the move she has been contemplating, Persenthein reveals his years of inattention: "Bist du denn nicht zufrieden? Sind wir denn nicht zufrieden?" (282).

The researcher's great difficulty in maintaining a satisfactory home life and yet working to capacity is further underscored by the number of novels in which any active romantic involvement for the main character is deferred until the research project, or at least the most demanding part of it, is concluded. In some cases, this postponement occurs naturally, because of the circumstances or the researcher's priorities. In other cases, the author uses a less convincing device to keep the chief character out of a potentially unresolvable conflict.

In *Viele sind berufen* Martin Bertram's female assistant and dear companion Genia leaves for parts unknown to conduct anthropological research before the most time-consuming and wearisome part of his experimentation.[12] She and Martin re-establish contact at the end of the novel, after he has reached his goal. In the last pages, there is a strong hint that the two will soon marry.

The author of *Shannon's Way* uses a slightly better device to keep Robert Shannon from being too distracted by romance while conducting the most grueling part of his research.[13] The parents of Jean Law, who helps Shannon with his project in its first phase, manage to keep her away from him (because of religious differences) until after the ironic conclusion of his project. Jean then decides for herself what she will do with her life. There is promise of a forthcoming wedding and a happy partnership, but the author ends the novel in time to avoid dealing directly with his hero's married life.

Richard Cameron in *The Undaunted* considers marriage only after he has confirmed his cure for pernicious anemia and presented his findings at a meeting of the American Medical Association. For a long time, due to his preoccupation with his work, he has not even realized his love for the young woman in question.

Similarly, Semmelweis in *The Cry and the Covenant* and *Retter der Mütter* takes time to socialize, fall in love, and marry only long after his research is finished and positive proof of his theory has been made public.[14]

Atypically, Fritz Wieser of *Die japanische Pest* is a happily married man throughout the novel. However, he conducts his research on a small Pacific island while his wife stays in Germany. Thus, except for showing the Wiesers' disagreement about the necessity for the central character's foreign adventure, the author avoids having to deal with the couple's home life.

Despite the many indications of the incompatibility of intensive medical research and matrimony, the subgenre does feature two marriages which without serious breaches withstand some of the worst emotional strains caused by the protagonists' research work. The two tenacious couples are Martin and Leora Arrowsmith, already mentioned in this context, and Henry and Liz Baker in *Medical Meeting*.[15]

The Arrowsmiths' marriage, until it is foreshortened by Leora's untimely death, has a much-tested resilience. Martin and Leora are married while he is in medical school, and her unshakable belief in him sustains them both through all but the last phase of his career, including periods of intensive research. Their relationship survives the great demands and privations of Martin's profession, his moodiness, his occasional identity crises and concomitant failures to appreciate Leora for what she is, and even his attraction to another woman.

The quality of the Arrowsmiths' relationship derives for the most part from the personal qualities of Leora, whose conception and characterization by Lewis have won praise from literary critics. This researcher's wife is loving, patient, loyal, and long-suffering, as revealed in this scene: "Leora was awaiting him—Leora whose fate it was ever to wait for him in creaky rocking-chairs in cheapish rooms. As he galloped in she smiled, and all her thin, sweet body was illumined" (269). She also has a closely related quality, indispensable in her association with Martin Arrowsmith and all the people she meets through him: "an immense power of accepting people as they were" (75). Cherishing "no especial personal ambition" but having "gay courage" and liking adventure (57), Leora makes a career of nurturing Martin's career and is able to put up with all the changes and uncertainties of their life together. She loves to serve, and there is a maternal quality about her. At one point, the narrator says, "She made him secure. She shut out the world that had pounded at him" (108). Martin realizes that Leora is for him "the source of life" (370). When Martin needs peace and quiet, she is serenely in the background; and during the long hours when Martin is not at home, she is "as easily and automatically contented by herself as a pussy cat" (220).

Leora is not, however, bland or shallow or subservient. She has spunk. When Martin fusses at her for taking so little care about her appearance and the impression she makes, she tells him, in effect, to take her as she is or not at all. Her devotion to Martin is neither selfless nor permissive. On one occasion, referring to his inclination toward a certain other young woman, she remarks, "I do want you to be happy, but unless I up and die on you some day, I'm not going to be hung up like an old cap. I warn you" (221).

In addition to the qualities necessary in a faithful and tenacious companion, Leora has a lustiness, an openness, and a genuineness that appeal to Martin. His first impression of Leora, summarized as follows, is never proven wrong:

> He felt an instant and complete comradeship with her, a relation free from...fencing and posing.... He knew that this girl was of his own people. If she was vulgar, jocular, unreticent, she was also gallant, she was full of laughter at humbugs, she was capable of a loyalty too casual and natural to seem heroic. (56)

Perhaps most important of all, however, is the fact that Leora not only understands what Martin's work is to him but also believes in it and in him. She is drawn to Martin in the first place largely because of his feeling for medical science. "I know your work is more important to you than I am, maybe more important than you are," she tells him, adding, "I simply admire you frightfully" (70). Sometimes, while Martin is busy in the laboratory, she sits silently by for long hours, apparently content just to be with him where he finds his fulfillment.

Leora's devotion is certainly more than Martin merits, considering how seldom he acknowledges her value to him. When he is moved to say, "I couldn't do anything without you!" (300), he is much closer to the truth than he usually comes. His earnest declaration, "I do love you so, even if this damned work does keep me tied up" (300), is essentially a confession of habitually taking her for granted. Though Martin loves Leora dearly, the normal level of his appreciation—at least while he works—is revealed in this observation of the narrator's: "Possibly the thing he most liked in Leora was her singular ability to be cheerfully non-existent even when she was present [in the laboratory]" (324).

Whether Leora is too good for Martin or not, she is apparently too good to last. In any case, Sinclair Lewis obviously considered Leora's cruel death from the plague necessary to the development of the novel. One might suspect that Lewis felt it impossible to let Martin have fulfilling research work and a lasting happy home life as well. Certainly, it is difficult to imagine Martin accomplishing his work at the end of the novel if he were living with any wife, even Leora. Married, he surely could not discover "the rapture of being allowed to work twenty-four hours a day without leaving an experiment at its juiciest moment to creep home for dinner" (426). Seen from another perspective, Leora's demise also lends the narrative a nice, realistic irony: because of her insistence on accompanying Martin on the St. Hubert expedition, she is separated from him forever. Overall, especially as one considers the outcome of Martin's second marriage, there seems to be an unwritten statement that the totally dedicated medical scientist cannot finally be held in the bonds of matrimony.

Mildred Walker, however, indicates just the opposite in her novel. Henry and Liz Baker, bound together by a love that has always been the envy of their friends, have worked together in their home laboratory for twelve years and have managed to rear a daughter in the midst of the research. Every time Henry has lost faith in his idea, Liz has reaffirmed her belief in him. Whenever Liz has lost patience with the unpleasant laboratory work and their poor life style, Henry's example has renewed her spirit and raised her ideals. Despite the difficulties, they have worked together as a team and held fast to each other.

Nevertheless, the blow dealt their project at the big medical meeting does cause a temporary crisis in their relationship. Liz, who has been looking forward to the payoff for all their hard work and self-denial, becomes understandably bitter about medical research. When someone compares her to Leora Arrowsmith, Liz comments, "She died, you remember, fairly early in his life. She might have grown tired of his working and working and not having anything to show for it eventually" (144).

To make matters worse, Liz finds out indirectly that their daughter's deafness was caused by the new drug that they have developed. Henry has never disclosed this fact to her. Liz is resentful and Henry is full of remorse, almost demoralized by events at the medical meeting.

In the end, however, their love and understanding prove stronger than this threat to their relationship. Each wants what is best for the other, and Liz discovers that she does not really want a "normal" way of life for them at the cost of their self-respect and sense of purpose.

There are two marriages—Robert Koch's second and Angela Koldewey's only one—which appear to be free of the typical strains, but even Koldewey's case reinforces the idea that a person cannot be properly devoted to medical research and to a spouse at the same time.[16] Koldewey, an anomaly in many ways, manages to avoid the usual problems of the researcher's home life by not mixing career and marriage. She renounces married life when she definitely decides on a career in medicine. She takes a husband only after she has chosen to give up research and medical practice because of her terminal illness.

As for Robert Koch's successful second marriage, all of the conditions are much better than a dedicated medical scientist could normally expect; and his wife is a very lucky find. Already established as a world-famous researcher, Koch has presumably adopted a fairly regular work schedule that will allow him time to be a husband. Moreover, since he has known both married life and its lack, he has doubtless resolved to put a considerable amount of effort into maintaining his second marriage. Koch is surely wiser after his experience with his first wife and marries a young woman whose outlook and stamina match his own. Unlike her predecessor, the second Mrs. Koch has a good idea of what she is getting into and presumably never has to worry about financial matters. It is also significant that she shares her husband's love of travel. She accompanies him on disease-fighting expeditions to far parts of the globe. She and the bacteriological work make Koch happy for the last seventeen years of his life.

Regardless of the fact that fictional medical researchers as a group have trouble fitting even their spouses into their lives, eight of the seventeen protagonists are parents by the end of their respective novels.[17] As one might expect, however, most of them are not very actively involved with their children. Indications of a main character's conscientiously fulfilling the responsibilities of parenthood—other than providing monetary support—are rare. In fact, one chief character, Georg Letham, seriously weighs the consequences in advance and decides against having a child. He admits being afraid of the responsibility, so afraid that by design he marries a woman too old to bear children (42). Three other central characters are also naturally protected against fatherhood, though without prior knowledge.[18] Understandably, medical research novels offer few scenes showing real interaction between protagonist and child. Furthermore, there are only four novels in which the child is developed as a character at all: *Medical Meeting, Helfer der Menschheit, Angela Koldewey,* and *Zwischenfall in Lohwinckel.*

Nevertheless, in some of the novels, children have a particular, if perhaps brief, importance: they provide the researchers an emotional outlet and cause them to rediscover life's simple joys. *The Cry and the Covenant* and *Retter der Mütter,* for example, depict the complete change that comes over a preoccupied and overworked scientist and physician when he is playing with a child. In *Helfer der Menschheit, Angela Koldewey,* and *Zwischenfall in Lohwinckel,* the main character is able to communicate with a child as with no other person.[19]

When Robert Koch is not lost in his work, he and his daughter Gertrud have a special rapport. She is his "getreuester Kamerad" (101) before he gets involved in microbiology. Later, Koch gives her all the love which he no longer gives his wife. Koch's letters to Gertrud when she is a grown woman are said to be "menschliche Dokumente von bleibendem Wert" (300).

Angela Koldewey and her son Volker are inseparable companions from the first moment of his life until she becomes too ill to take care of him. Volker, an angelic counterpart to Pearl in Nathaniel Hawthorne's *Scarlet Letter*, somehow senses his mother's coming death before he is told anything about it. After he indicates what he knows, Angela talks to him on the subject of dying though she cannot do so with anyone else.

Rehle, the precocious daughter of the taciturn and unfriendly Nikolas Persenthein, often accompanies him on his rounds and is at times his sole confidante. She understands and accepts him as no one else does—even her mother.

Notwithstanding all benefits of having children, only one chief character, Angela Koldewey, is a consistently good parent—and for only a limited time, at that. The others, usually either engrossed in research or busy caring for patients, just do not have the time for much active involvement with their children. Henry Baker, for example, though a loving and concerned father, is seldom available for any recreation with his wife Liz and their daughter Nancy. Liz and Nancy quite often have to eat meals without him and sometimes do not see him for thirty-six hours at a time. The worst example of a parent is Martin Arrowsmith, who, as mentioned earlier, abandons his wife Joyce and their little son. When Joyce makes the appeal to his conscience, "And our son is to be left without your care?" he callously replies, "Would he have my care if I died?" (429). Even Robert Koch, whose love for his daughter Gertrud is said to have the greatness characteristic of all his passions (100), pays his child only superficial and infrequent attention during the most intensive period of his research.

Like the bonds of matrimony and parenthood, the central characters' bonds to their original families tend to be weakened by their involvement in medical research. To be sure, most of the novelists seem to see the relationships to parents, brothers, sisters, and other relatives as either bothersome topics or details which clutter the portrait of the researcher unless relegated to the distant background. While many of the narrators acknowledge the influence of the protagonist's heritage and childhood home, few of them show or tell of any contact between the scientist and his or her parents.[20] In most of the novels, the parents are either dead or just not mentioned after the doctor becomes a researcher. As for siblings, cousins, uncles and aunts, etc., most of the main characters either have none or else just never communicate with them.[21]

The protagonist's in-laws are featured as minor characters in four novels—*Arrowsmith, Narkose, Zwischenfall in Lohwinckel,* and *The Cry and the Covenant.* Only in *Narkose,* however, does the main character have any dealings with his wife's family during the period of time when he is conducting research.[22] Morton even takes eleven days off from his experimentation and dental practice to search for his wife's sister's husband, who is a fugitive from justice.

If most of the chief characters have little time for family, they have less for friends—except, of course, those with whom they can talk about their work. As for close friends, eleven of the central characters end up having no one of their own sex with whom they share an affection that goes beyond the mutual appreciation of fellow professionals and with whom they somewhat regularly spend leisure time.[23] The five characters who are best friends of protagonists—after the latter have become medical researchers—are, understandably, colleagues.[24]

Except where the narrator states or implies otherwise, one may assume that any given main character has had at least one close friend at some time before becoming involved in medical research. However, such old friends are rarely mentioned in the novels. There are very few really longtime friends with whom the researchers remain in contact. The chief characters' associations with people not somehow connected with medical science lose their importance to them or at least to the novelists.

Medical Meeting by Mildred Walker shows what happens to one researcher's friendships and his sociability over a period of years. Henry Baker and his wife Liz find that they no longer have much in common with their good friends from medical school days and never will have much of a bond with their current closest associates. All of the Bakers' friends, though they are physicians and their wives, are outsiders with respect to medical research. And while Henry and Liz have been investing so much of themselves in Henry's project, the four other couples have become interested in security, prestige, and the making and spending of money.

Henry, the assistant to the superintendent of a state sanitarium for tuberculars, has for the last twelve years been dividing his time between his job and work on a tuberculostat that he has produced from a species of mold. Liz has been helping him in the laboratory and taking care of their home and child. They have not had the time or even the desire for the society of others: "Henry's work had held them so tightly together that they hadn't needed other people" (81).

Their only social contacts now are the sanitarium's superintendent, Carl Dalton, and his wife Hester; and the occasional evenings at the Daltons' are essentially command performances. The visit depicted at the beginning of the novel reveals that there is no deep friendship between the two couples. Because the Bakers are so different from the Daltons, they do not feel at ease with them. Carl completely lacks Henry's creativity, intensity, and drive to achieve. He is satisfied with his routine job, which gives him prominence in a small town, enough money to live quite comfortably, and enough free time to play poker. Hester enjoys the finer things of life and rather pities Liz, who because of Henry's small salary cannot even seriously aspire to refinements. At the same time, however, Hester envies Liz her close association with the work of a man of promise.

The big medical meeting in Chicago brings the Bakers back together with their old friends, whom they have not actually seen since the men were in medical school together. The conversations there reveal how much the priorities of everyone except Liz and Henry have changed. Liz remembers how they all "used to argue about medical things" and observes to herself, "Now they were talking about personalities, and positions and possessions" (58-59). She is eager to be asked about Henry's research, since he is the only one of the group who is presenting a paper; but no one seems genuinely interested in it. Liz finds that the dinner conversation on the first night is like the ice cream: "It had a sweet, flat taste and it was lukewarm" (59). There is, of course, some real communication within this group, but Liz muses at the end of the medical meeting that she and Henry somehow don't seem to know the others as well as they did before seeing them again (227).

Arrowsmith shows the deterioration of one medical scientist's seemingly very close friendship with someone who is not involved in medical research. Late in the novel, Martin remembers his former roommate Clif Clawson as the "best friend a man ever had" (407) though the two have seen each other only twice since medical school. Clif, who was expelled from the school, has become a drifter and salesman and schemer while Martin has become a medical scientist. After fourteen years, crude and unimproved Clif drops in on Martin at work and embarrasses him. Martin invites Clif to dinner just so as not to be guilty of disloyalty to an old friend, and this last meeting makes it clear that they now inhabit worlds that are hopelessly foreign to each other.

Alex Addams laments the passing of the general feeling of amiability that he enjoyed in his youth. Although he seems to have more time for a social life than most other protagonists, he has come to feel alienated from most people within as well as without his profession. He asks himself, "Among all those I now work or play with, is there one I could go to, count as a friend?" and answers, "Suspicion, ambition, competition underlie all approaches, all relations" (16). For him, at least at his emotional low point, the world has become devoid of friendliness (16).

Addams' problem is, however, largely of his own making. He does find very sympathetic comrades in fellow researchers Hans Kohn and Sidney MacBride, and he fondly remembers his fatherly former professor and colleague Gustav Brenner, but his reserve will not allow him to commit himself completely in friendship. He is courteous and cordial in his way, he is brilliant and articulate, but he seldom expresses his inner self to another man. It is clear throughout the novel that he is a superachiever who abhors failure and does not like being in a position of weakness in any area of his life. At the research institute, the "reassuring and peaceful place" (22) where he has "failed no one" (15), he is able to enjoy a certain amount of companionship; but nowhere, except in a heterosexual liaison, will he risk vulnerability to the extent necessary for real communion.

Some other protagonists have never had any very close friendships in the first place. This lack, of course, is primarily due to their personalities and the kinds of interests they have pursued, both factors indicating something about the general type of person who becomes a dedicated researcher.

Robert Koch, whose social life is virtually non-existent once he commences his research, is said to have had few friends as a boy. The narrator of *Helfer der Menschheit* explains, "Er ist ihnen zu sehr überlegen, zu erwachsen, zu ernst, auch zu arbeitsbesessen und phantastisch" (40). As a medical scientist to whom very little matters other than his warfare against disease, Koch is essentially a loner. He can be friendly enough to his closest colleagues, but none of them is a close friend. "Keiner war im Umgang mit Menschen so wählerisch wie er," comments the narrator (198). Although as a country doctor he is in a lively social circle, Koch is basically shy and reserved with strangers (87). Rather than becoming more gregarious and expansive with increasing fame, Koch becomes more modest, retiring, and inaccessible:

Je populärer der Name des grossen Forschers in der Welt wird, je mehr sich Philanthropen, ehrgeizige Mitarbeiter und Freunde an ihn herandrängen, der jetzt auf der Höhe seines Ruhmes steht, um so einsamer wird der Mann selbst, um so anspruchsloser und verschlossener. (299)

Hans Lennhoff in *Die Spur* is also a shy, reserved person who has never had an intimate friend. With a bent for investigation but little inclination to form lasting attachments, he has pursued science rather than friendships. Besides, being immersed in his schooling and then in his mission to defeat Palang-Negah fever, he has not had time for recreation and personal relationships.

Lennhoff's work might also be seen as a protection against intimate involvements with other people. Busy in his laboratory, Lennhoff remains oblivious to virtually everything in the world outside—for example, "Mord, Brand, Liebe, Verzweiflung" (10). The narrator's association of love and despair here is conspicuous, as is his inclusion of *Liebe* in a list of things which one might well wish never to experience. At any rate, Lennhoff's laboratory is a quiet sanctuary where personal relationships and attendant personal problems do not—indeed, must not—enter.

Josef Zeppichmann of *The Fire and the Wood* has no friends for many of the same reasons. At first, his idea of fulfillment has nothing to do with other people. Working full time as a doctor and conducting his research at home at night, he feels that he has no time for friends. He hates the thought of "spending time and getting nothing for it" (114). He enjoys the mental picture of himself spending "long evenings at his bench there, hundreds of hours of contented patience" (16). "To work as Koch did," Josef thinks, "alone and utterly confident: that was happiness" (16). Besides, as mentioned elsewhere, there is little about Josef to attract others to him.

Apparently, he has never had a very significant friendship, but he does come to realize what he has been missing. The question is exactly how and when he will go about filling this void in his life:

Friends, that was what he wanted: the peculiar sense of unity which friends seemed to have. As yet he hadn't grasped the trick of it, but later, when his great experiment was done and he was famous, Josef would learn the trick and get some. (140-141)

Unlike Zeppichmann, Nikolas Persenthein seems not even to want friends—at least, once his *Idee* has set him against established medical science and the town in which he lives. The townspeople of Lohwinckel have no confidence in him and his strange methods, and "bissige Feindschaft" has grown out of "einer lächelnden Missachtung" (23). Patients are afraid of the preoccupied, ill-tempered, and impatient doctor (24). For his part, Persenthein feels that he must remain "hart und ruhelos" (25).

While a career in medical science, in combination with certain personal characteristics, keeps most of the main characters from having any intimate friends, this occupation also provides many with opportunities to form one or more new close relationships. These close relationships follow four patterns: in five novels, a colleague becomes the chief character's best friend; in three novels, a filial attachment to an older researcher develops;[25] in some cases, a co-worker or the spouse of one becomes simply a close friend (of neither type above); and in more than half of the cases, the central character meets someone of the opposite sex with whom he or she falls in love.

The best friends are diverse in personality but are all in some sense co-workers of the protagonists. Terry Wickett, Martin Arrowsmith's best friend at the end of the novel, is easy-going, uninhibited, and socially unrefined; but he is well-educated, very strict, and unforgiving as a scientist. When Martin starts to work at the McGurk Institute, Terry is already a full-time researcher there as well as a close associate of Max Gottlieb. Martin Bertram's best friend Wendemuth is very stiff, reserved and aloof from most of his fellow doctor-scientists at the research institute where Martin comes to work. Said to resemble Robespierre, Wendemuth is a haughty fanatic in his personal as well as professional life. Georg Letham's companion March is sensitive, considerate, jocular, sensual, and homosexual. Despite Letham's assertion of being able to give wholehearted love to his work only and not to any person (465), he calls March his first true friend (400). March comes to mean more to Letham than Letham's brother (474), but his erotic attraction to the main character is not reciprocated. A quick and willing learner though not a trained scientist, March becomes a very valuable, hard-working laboratory assistant to Letham and the other two doctors on the yellow fever project. Semmelweis' best friend Markussovsky is sensitive, intelligent, generous, and all that a young gentleman of noble birth should be. As related in Note 24 of this chapter, he is a doctor (but not a researcher) who does much to help Semmelweis' cause. Neil Spence, the best friend of Robert Shannon, is very shy and quiet, serious to the point of being melancholy, but also very courteous, kind, and undemanding. Since a deformity from a war injury has left him unable to pursue a private medical practice, he is a full-time researcher in the same laboratory where Shannon embarks upon his project.

An older colleague in research becomes almost a father figure for Alex Addams, Martin Arrowsmith, and Georg Letham.[26] Addams' and Arrowsmith's former professors, Brenner and Gottlieb respectively, take such interest in their brightest students' careers that personal relationships develop. As students, Addams and Arrowsmith are glad of the older men's help, advice, and recognition of their talents. In both cases, the elder is the embodiment of the younger man's scientific ideals and is a lovable eccentric. Letham's filial affection for his last remaining research teammate, Carolus, develops under such extreme conditions that either fast friendship or bitter hatred would seem inevitable. In the last phase of their yellow fever project, the two live and work together in very close quarters and must contend with agonizing boredom as well as great physical and emotional discomfort. Their friendship is the product of mutual professional respect, unwavering commitment to the same goal, and their common need for companionship and moral support. Their age difference, though not as great as that in either of the other two cases, accounts for the quasi father-son relationship.

All of the other close friends of chief characters are either directly involved in medical science or somehow connected with it. *Arrowsmith's* Gustav Sondelius is successively Martin's hero, co-worker, travel companion, and beloved comrade in arms in the battle against the plague epidemic. Hans Hühnerdieb, toward whom Martin Bertram comes to feel like an older brother, is a medical student who becomes the central character's devoted assistant and apartment mate. Ellen, the wife of Bertram's best friend and fellow researcher Wendemuth, also becomes a dear friend of the protagonist. Sandy Farquhar, whom Richard Cameron befriends, is a doctor and scientist in the field of radiology. Joe DiPallo, who becomes almost like a brother to Cameron, has been his helper, housemate, and experimental subject. Semmelweis' valued friend Ferdinand Hebra is first his professor, and Johann Chiari is a colleague who was once a fellow medical student. Any others who could be considered Semmelweis' intimates are also doctors.

Medical research work provides a favorable setting for intimacy of another sort as well. On the job, Addams, Arrowsmith, Bertram, Cameron, Kalsten, Koldewey, Lennhoff, Letham, Shannon, Töpfer, and Zeppichmann each make a consequential acquaintance of a member of the opposite sex.[27] And amorous impulses, not unlikely to occur when a man and a woman in any setting are in each other's company a great deal and share an active commitment to a cause, prompt all of these main characters except Lennhoff and Töpfer to become romantically involved with their new companions. Arrowsmith, Cameron, Koldewey, and Zeppichmann marry theirs; and Bertram, Kalsten, and Shannon become engaged before the end of their respective novels. The other two chief characters are not fortunate in love: Addams' passionate laboratory assistant becomes interested in someone else, and Letham's beautiful young patient dies.

Addams, Arrowsmith, Lennhoff, and Töpfer are married when their work brings each of them together with a companionable young woman, and these new relationships range from torridly erotic to strictly professional. By definition, only Addams' and Arrowsmiths' new affiliations, which eventually lead to deep involvement, are close ones; however, the other two merit mention here because of what they reveal about the medical scientists.

Interestingly enough, Addams' and Arrowsmith's strong feelings for the new women in their lives do not make any difference in their marriages. Addams, who has an earnest, sexually intensive love affair with his laboratory assistant Irene until she leaves him for another man, is already separated from his wife. For Martin Arrowsmith and Joyce Lanyon (a wealthy landowner turned volunteer during the plague epidemic), no real romance develops right away despite their instant and almost narcissistic attraction to each other. Furthermore, this new affinity has no chance of causing Martin strife at home because his wife Leora, whom he still loves as much as ever, dies of the plague at about the time that he, in another town, meets Joyce.

The two more platonic new acquaintanceships reveal the monogomous and very businesslike nature of Walter Töpfer and Hans Lennhoff. Töpfer does not allow anything untoward to happen between him and his extremely helpful colleague Martha Wilfried, but he notices certain difficulties in working closely with her. Agitated by suspicions of her feelings for him and subconsciously fearing his feelings for her, he abruptly stops their research collaboration. Ironically, Hans Lennhoff's quite innocent relationship with his laboratory assistant Hanna Weber contributes to a permanent marital rift. As already noted, his resentful and envious wife Renate stops speaking to him, and their unfortunate marriage heads unimpeded toward legal dissolution. Although Lennhoff's excellent new assistant admires him greatly and is young, unattached, and pretty, the dedicated researcher simply does not notice or consider the potential for a love affair with her. He is fond of Hanna personally and much impressed by her professionally, but he keeps his mind on his work. As for Hanna, she does not allow herself to think about her feelings for Lennhoff as a man because she knows that it would be pointless to fall in love with such a single-minded researcher. The author of *Die Spur* creates the almost perfect conditions for a laboratory romance perhaps to tease his readers and certainly to show what his hero is made of.

Although most of the new relationships with members of the opposite sex distract the central characters from their work somewhat, all of them decidedly profit the research. Most of the new partners provide valuable moral support and help the researchers with the experimentation itself. Arrowsmith's and Bertram's new loves help them financially.[28]

The one exceptional relationship of this kind is that of Georg Letham and the earlier mentioned teenage girl dying of yellow fever. Here the significant benefit is indirect. Though Letham's deep affection for his precious *kleine Portugiesin* is doubly futile, just discovering his capacity to love is immeasurably valuable to him. Seeing the girl dying makes Letham appreciate the absolute worth of every human life. And her death ultimately contributes to his personal motivation in the fight against yellow fever.

Unfortunately, medical research also provides specific occasions for two of the protagonists to lose friends. As mentioned earlier, Martin Arrowsmith's good friend and colleague Gustav Sondelius dies of the plague while working with him during the epidemic. Georg Letham's esteemed colleague Walter sacrifices his life in the team's yellow fever experiment. Although Letham has not been able to develop a close relationship with Walter, he has always been very fond of him. And while losing Walter, Letham unintentionally drives away his best friend March. March, who has been associated with medical science only in order to stay close to Letham, is horrified by the use of Walter's wife as an unsuspecting experimental subject and begins to hate Letham for his heartlessness.

It has been seen that a given main character's medical research work may nurture or undermine a close relationship with another person, depending on common interests, the personalities involved, and the nature and strength of the individuals' commitment to each other. Typically, the fictional medical researcher, introverted, reserved, absorbed in his or her work and inclined to discount emotions, has very few lasting close relationships with other people. Some of the chief characters have never had strong connections outside the family, and many appear to be without living relatives. For the majority of them, longtime affiliations—those with parents, siblings, other relatives, or friends—fade in significance, except in the few cases where the other person has some connection to medical science. In two of the novels, more recent friendships are lost because of medical research. In the novels as a whole, total commitment to medical science is usually incompatible with a strong, lasting marriage; and it appears virtually impossible for the devoted researcher to be a consistently good parent. On the other hand, the central character typically owes at least one very important new acquaintance to his or her profession. Certainly, any new close relationships which last are either with co-workers or with persons very supportive of the protagonist's work. Thus, the medical research profession, which is a detriment to many relationships, is figuratively a fertile soil for others.

Chapter Five
Attitudes Toward Social Issues,
Culture, and Recreation

Most of the authors appear to face a dilemma with regard to their protagonists' outside interests—interests in economics, politics, culture, and recreation.[1] They want to demonstrate their main characters' power of concentration and dedication to research, yet they want to make these medical scientists "broad" enough to be interesting and sympathetic. Although almost half of the authors indicate that "breadth" in the medical scientist is not important as long as sufficient depth of character has been established, the rest of the novelists attempt somehow to give their chief characters both.

The problem for the researchers is, of course, finding enough spare time and energy to devote to extraprofessional activities. Even so, the majority cultivate at least one outside interest during some break in their work. And about a third of them are concerned enough about a social issue to take action personally to protect an individual or a group from unfair treatment.

The following illustrations show fictional medical researchers' various levels of interest and involvement in the general human affairs and pursuits that concern this chapter. The first case study, that of Josef Zeppichmann, depicts the extreme of non-involvement. Zeppichmann's sketch is the most detailed because his detachment from the major social and political issues of his time is so remarkable under the circumstances. He is representative of only a minority of the protagonists, but his case sheds light on most others by means of contrast.

At the beginning of *The Fire and the Wood*, Josef Zeppichmann's only major concern is that he be able to verify and then demonstrate the importance of his medical discovery.[2] Young Zeppichmann, who has just acquired his Dr. med. degree, has been working for about six years to develop a new polyvalent tuberculin and now needs to test it on a human subject. Although he is meticulous in performing his official duties as assistant house surgeon at a general hospital, he has no feeling for the patients, as mentioned previously. His immediate supervisor, though unable to find fault with Josef's work, complains that Josef is too narrow and "ought to have some other interest, some philosophy" (35). The older doctor sums up most people's objections to Josef thus: "A man ought to be a human being, when all's said and done" (35).

Working single-mindedly toward his goal, Josef remains willfully unaware of everything except his job and his project. He has no friends and, at first, seeks none. The opposite sex, which he considers irrational, does not interest him. For the present, Josef attaches little importance to such matters as charm, tact, or his personal appearance. His only concern with culture is trying to shed all vestiges of his provincial upbringing and make people recognize him as an educated man of great capabilities. He allows himself little relaxation during his twenty to twenty-one waking hours per day, and apparently, his only diversion is scanning the newspaper infrequently and aimlessly. At meals, so as not to waste time, he usually reads medical literature which relates to his project. Sometimes he works through mealtime.

The author emphasizes Josef's total dedication to his research project by showing this young Jewish doctor's indifference to the universally significant political events of the early 1930s in Germany. Josef declares emphatically, "I never meddle with politics. I've too much else to think about" (14). He remains far too long unaware of the danger awaiting all Jews in Germany, and then he hopes to avoid trouble by ignoring it. He appears to have little concern for his people—indeed, for people in general—and wants only to be left alone to conclude his experiment.

Apparently, Josef thinks about his family and former neighbors only when he has just received a letter from home; and even then, he is primarily fantasizing about how these people will be impressed by his fame and social respectability. He remembers the smallness, the hardness, the poverty, and the ugliness of his home town and does not plan to return for a visit until he can show how successful and completely refined he has become. He shudders at the thought of being trapped in medical practice there.

Since Josef envisions his cure for tuberculosis eventually saving millions of lives, he is at first willing to sacrifice everything to his research. Like the unnamed politician whose speech he has seen in a newspaper, Josef is so intent on his goal that he has deluded himself into thinking, "The individual does not matter" (74, 80). Later, however, he will discover what it feels like to be one of the millions of individuals who do not matter to the Nazi regime.

In the meantime, despite Josef's attitude toward other people and their concerns, he finds himself one evening in the company of his young colleague Dr. Ahlwarth and this man's radical friends. These people discuss social, economic, and political conditions which Josef has preferred to ignore since finding a higher purpose in life. Josef wants to leave when the radicals start discussing plans to avenge the recent disabling of a comrade, but he feels pressured into contributing to their bomb fund before he goes. His false generosity draws a rebuke from Ahlwarth, who knows that any blow against the Nazis will bring brutal retaliation. When Ahlwarth accuses him of being insensitive to the real needs of the poor, Josef replies, "I am not unsympathetic with poor people, I lived among them for many years" (128). Then, taking his leave, he vows to himself never to "waste an evening on social exercises again" (129).

However, though Alwarth's friends are alien to Josef and their political philosophy is lost on him, he has been impressed by their *Kameradschaft* and their sense of common purpose. Afterward, seeing them about to be attacked by a group of young Nazi toughs, he alerts them. He then jumps between one of the radicals and a pursuer and gets his collar bone broken for his trouble. Having made this sacrifice, Josef feels a strange new gratification.

This pleasure notwithstanding, he is not about to get directly involved in politics or trouble himself about current events in his country. He is only vaguely aware of "fragments belonging to a world outside his own, bits of conversation...heard in the Staff Mess, newspaper headings" and has considered this information "no concern of a scientist with his job to do" (191). After receiving a letter from his father urging him to come home to avoid rigorous enforcement of the new regulations for Jews, Josef is interested only in avoiding humiliation: he hates the thought of returning home without having succeeded as a researcher. And even after being summarily dismissed from his position at the hospital, he is anxious about only one thing—finishing his experiment so that he can publish his results before he runs out of money. A related concern also helps keep Josef's mind off matters of politics and ethnicity: he has become very fond of Minna, the subject of his experiment. Keeping her alive now matters to him personally and not just for the sake of his research.

Even Josef's own personal experience of anti-Semitism fails to sensitize him to the great trouble that has befallen the Jews in Germany. His reactions to the indignity of being forcibly prevented from tending an Aryan accident victim show that he still thinks there is no real problem if he chooses to ignore it:

As he made his way back through the crowd he saw they were staring at him intently, some without malice. But he did not bother about that. His rage, while it lasted, was a coat of armour against such curiosity, and his lips were smiling. He thought, "Well, she can die, if that's how they want it. It's not my business, she belongs to them." (212-213)

When he can no longer ignore the danger which awaits him, a Jew and now a suspected communist, Josef still spends no time thinking about politics or the plight of his people. Even as men enter his room to arrest him, he thinks of nothing except the safety of his research notes and the health of Minna. However, he is forced to leave without doing much about either.

While Josef is a prisoner in labor camps, he is conscious of little more than his immediate surroundings. The narrator never indicates that Josef thinks about the political situation or worries about German Jewry or even the people in his home town. Everything in Josef's past except his acquaintance with Minna seems to belong to a separate life that he can barely remember.

During Josef and Minna's flight from Germany (after she has arranged his rescue), Josef is too sick and too broken in spirit to worry about anything except Minna's well-being and the safe delivery of his research notes to some benevolent medical authority. He tells Minna, "It doesn't matter about me, only you mustn't let them [the Nazis] steal the book" (379). His only concern for the ethno-politics of the situation is that his being a Jew may damage his scientific credibility: "You needn't tell them [foreign doctors] it was me, don't tell them it was me who did all that. They'd say it wasn't any use, they'd say a Jew couldn't think of anything to do people any good" (378).

The humble, somewhat aware Josef Zeppichmann at the end of the novel is radically different from the hard, brash, egocentric young man of the beginning. Although his level of ethnic consciousness and social activism may be unacceptable to American readers of the 1990s, he has at least come to terms with his ethnic identity. And if Josef never develops an outside interest (other than his love for Minna) or embraces a philosophy as his supervisor would have had him do, at least he has reordered his priorities. He still values his medical research work most highly, but he is finally interested in the conquest of tuberculosis for its own sake and not for his self-enhancement. He is no longer willing to sacrifice any other individual's welfare to that conquest. Having suffered much at the hands of ruthless visionaries, he now refuses to let anybody else suffer for the sake of his medical goal.

Henry Baker of *Medical Meeting* is another central character who has no time for an interest in politics, philosophy, cultural matters, or the like.[3] Although the narrator makes references to World War II and other international topics of the day, Henry and his wife Liz do not discuss current world affairs—except happenings in medicine—at any time in the novel. As for cultural enrichment, they have not been able to spare any time or money for it. During the twelve years Henry has spent on his research project, he has seldom even left the sanitarium grounds where he lives and works. Liz and Henry's trip to the big medical meeting where he reports his results is their first outing of more than a day in length since the beginning of the research project. Nevertheless, Henry has no regrets about what his work has caused him to miss. When Liz remarks how hard he has worked for so many years and for so little compensation, he says, "I didn't want to do anything else, really" (34).

Angela Koldewey also has no important outside interests during the time when she is working on her research project.[4] When she takes a walk or skis, it is primarily to renew her strength for her work. She tells her would-be suitor that she does not seek diversion for its own sake because she feels guilty about any time she spends away from her work: "Können Sie ermessen, wie ich wegen jeder Zeit, die ich nicht an meiner Arbeit verbringe, ein Schuldgefühl habe?" (104).

Another researcher with very much the same feeling for his work is Hans Lennhoff, whose virtual isolation from the world outside his laboratory has been mentioned already in other contexts.[5] He knows that he has become very one-sided, but he feels that the importance of his work demands such sacrifice: "Natürlich wurde man einseitig dabei. Wann hatte er zum letztenmal ein gutes Buch gelesen? Aber war nicht auch das Palang-Negah-Fieber eine einseitige Angelegenheit, eine verdammt einseitige sogar?" (161). In only one instance does he express real regret for missing so much of the enjoyment of life. Taking a rare walk with his wife in a park, he observes, "Schön ist das—und ist eine Sünde gegen den lieben Gott, dass ich noch kein einziges Mal hier entlanggekommen bin" (127). Later, however, he realizes how much more his work means to him than does the pursuit of pleasure. Aside from his honeymoon, which combines research-related activities with leisure, Lennhoff takes only one trip for enjoyment and relaxation: when rest from his work becomes a medical imperative, he goes to visit a colleague in England. Lennhoff's only other voyage, just begun at the very end of the novel, is to take him to the site of the second phase of his research project.

Nikolas Persenthein in *Zwischenfall in Lohwinckel* does his best to keep the affairs of the world and specifically those of his own community from distracting him from his research work, but he finds himself forced to take a moral stand when the order and security of his own household are threatened.[6] Persenthein has very few concerns in common with his fellow townspeople. He takes no part in local politics and is not perturbed by the local gossip—even when the topic is the Persentheins' own finances or their alleged extramarital romantic interests. He takes an active part in what could be called an environmental issue only because of its medical-scientific interest to him: having determined that workers in the local battery factory have a tremendously higher incidence of lead poisoning than the rest of the populace, Persenthein calls in an occupational health inspector to force corrective measures in the factory. But later, when general unrest and disorder troubles the town, he wants only to shut it out of his inner world: " 'Arbeiten', dachte er wieder, es war Flucht und Egoismus in dem Gedanken und der heftige Wunsch, die Unruhe nicht in die eigensten Bezirke, in die Welt der Idee eindringen zu lassen" (250). Unfortunately, his wife has fallen prey to dissatisfaction and extreme restlessness and wants to leave him for another man. No longer able to ignore what is happening to the town, Persenthein makes an eloquent—though private—plea for moral duty and the inviolability of marriage:

Das Sittliche, das Sittliche ist ja immer das Unangenehme und das Schwere. Kämpfen, Überwinden, Verzichten, Entsagen, Sichbeherrschen—da hast du die Dinge, die auf der Seite des Sittlichen stehen. Die Ehe steht auf dieser Seite; die Treue auch. Das andere— ich verstehe, wie verlockend es ist. Aber es passt nicht zu uns, Elisabeth. (286)

Just one step removed from the protagonists who remain essentially oblivious to the world beyond their wards and laboratories, or attempt to remain so, is Georg Letham.[7] During the main part of his narrative, Letham does not leave the quarantined hospital where he and others are conducting yellow fever research. Furthermore, he does not care about what is happening outside the hospital grounds. Much earlier in the novel, however, Letham does mention two avocations, both of which are unique to this novel.

As the narrator of his own story, Letham says in the prologue that he has undertaken the writing of his memoirs as an experiment, perhaps his last. He expresses the wish to produce "ein alle Menschengehirne erleuchtendes Kunstwerk" as well as documentation (8). He tells his story with psychological and sociological insights deeper than those of any other main character.

In his first chapter, Letham mentions another interest not directly related to medical science: he likes to gamble and is generally quite successful at it. Gambling is both a needed diversion from his laboratory work and a source of financing for his costly experiments. Letham says that his activities in the laboratory and the casino complement each other quite well: "Ich habe mich mit Arbeit betäubt, wenn ich des Spielens müde war, und mich mit Spiel betäupt, wenn ich der geistigen Arbeit nicht mehr mit der nötigen Spannkraft und Konzentration gewachsen war" (12). While playing baccarat, Letham also gets new ideas for laboratory procedures.

Richard Cameron, though not as intellectual as Georg Letham, seems to care more about the world outside his medical domain.[8] During a lull in his research activity, Cameron spends some time probing art and philosophy to learn the meaning of life. This search is prompted by three things: a difficult question in professional ethics, subconscious distress over his temporary lack of new ground to break, and guilt feelings from his many years of thinking of "little but narrowly personal and professional matters" (292). Unfortunately, he finds no satisfying answers in the cynical films, stage productions, and fiction of the day. Nor do philosophical works give him what he wants. Philosophy repels him because he is "searching for a way to live, not for a theory of relativity" (292). The narrator says that the central character "floundered in the shallows of contemporary thought," adding that "however great the depths might be farther out, he could not reach them" (292).

Not the arts or formal philosophy but a bit of folk wisdom retained from medical school helps Cameron rediscover his purpose in life. He remembers hearing, "The amount of water you can get out of a well depends not so much on the well as on the size of your cup" (292) and satisfies himself that the size of his proverbial cup has determined his proper pursuit. What gives his life meaning and allows him to maintain equilibrium is challenging and absorbing research work. He resolves, "I'm going to leave the problems of the universe to chaps who enjoy fog and moonshine and have bigger cups" (292).

It is significant that in making his philosophical inquiries, Cameron does not seek the aid of counselors, seminars, or organizations of any kind. He goes his own way, in the company of his wife Judith. He remains true to the credo he has stated earlier: "I'm not a joiner. The fewer things I belong to, the fewer strings there are on me for people to pull" (112).

Cameron does not, on the other hand, exhibit narrowness of vision throughout most of the novel. Although there are periods of time when he can think of nothing but developing a cure for pernicious anemia, he is in general quite aware of the greater world around him. His passion for exploring, which is the primary motivation in his research, makes him attend to his surroundings and probe with his mind and yearn to travel. When he is out of doors, he takes notice of the works of nature, as when he decries cities' pollution of streams. Having been, among other things, a military medic in France during World War I and a country doctor in Montana, he has seen different ways of life with which to compare his own. At times, he expresses himself on the subject of Americanism. And although he is ordinarily "but little inclined to think of philosophical abstractions" (290), Cameron philosophizes on a fairly wide range of subjects, including romance and war.

Furthermore, Cameron is not loath to get personally involved in righting an injustice. He actively takes the part of his friend Sandy Farquhar, a latent homosexual radiologist who is continually harassed and suppressed professionally. Through comments made by Cameron, Farquhar, and the narrator, the author makes the chief character, by extension, a defender of the rights of all of society's black sheep.

Alex Addams is quite a different sort of person from Richard Cameron, but the two researchers have similarities important here.[9] Like Cameron, Addams is concerned and well-informed about the world and given to philosophizing. Although he suspects that scientists develop their "peculiar curiosity" at the expense of "interest in human beings" and wonders, "Why does it not concern me that I do not know what my neighbors say and feel?" (13), he is, like Cameron, willing to act on his principles to protect the rights of another.

Having been powerless to stop the Foundation's groundless dismissal of a German-American scientist during the World War I era, Addams uses his now considerable leverage at this research institute to keep the same kind of injustice from being done to a German Jewish colleague in the mid-1930s. By threatening to resign if Hans Kohn is fired, Addams is able to save the job of this friend, whose political views and ethnic heritage make him undesirable to the director. Later, Addams offers to sacrifice his own teaching salary in order to secure a raise for Kohn.

Addams seems to have a lot more time and opportunity than most other main characters for grappling with moral questions and pondering cultural matters. Usually engaged in theoretical rather than "practical" medical science, Addams is conditioned to consider the broadest implications of any given set of facts. In particular, he philosophizes a lot about human sexuality, American society in the 1930s, and the future of democracy. He also enjoys discussing "Jewishness" with his friend Kohn.

Although Addams insists that he has no interest in politics, he keeps abreast of world events of the time and cannot keep from having political opinions. As a researcher, he thinks that he should be above, or at least removed from, politics because "even in the midst of revolutionary disturbance scientists should continue; they must preserve and cultivate the invaluable harvest they have been gathering for centuries" (104). The narrator comments, "Social or political thought in action, when he glimpsed it, appeared to him for the most part comtemptibly confused alongside the ordered vision and progress of science" (65). And yet Addams is not at all indifferent to the political scene in his country. He states his dislike of World War I and its "jingoes" (117), and he calls the present revolutionary spirit of some people around him "premature" and "abortive" (104).

Wanting to maintain objectivity, Addams tries to stay neutral in the conflict between radicalism and reaction. The author dramatizes Addams' position by having him happen upon a strikers' demonstration which has turned into a bloody battle with police. When Addams offers his medical services to the wounded, he finds himself "an outsider in this conflict" though either side may make use of him (331).

In the course of the novel, however, Addams comes to see how hard it is for a scientist of his prominence and in his situation to remain politically uninvolved. His research institute becomes polarized when many of the employees want to form a labor union and the administration starts to repress those who preach radical ideas. Addams' estranged wife Louise, a patroness of revolution though a member of the Foundation's board of trustees, warns Addams that "in the fight which is raging now there are no more civilians" (388). She says, "All are forced to take part, an aggressive part. If you withdraw you are destroyed or you rot" (388).

Still determined that he will spend his time on his work and not on political activism, Addams thinks seriously of leaving the Foundation. He is not greatly moved when Louise urges him to stay and help her to keep the doors open for all non-committed scientists like himself and for those who are preparing to fight for the preservation of what he represents (388). "I will stay," he decides, "not because I believe in revolution but because of my faith in science and in freedom" (389).

Addams sees virtually no limit to what knowledgeable, rational people can achieve in a democratic society. For example, he believes that the "vicious civil war" between labor and management in the United States could be ended (331-332). He says, "The country is crowded with wise political and social scientists" (332) and adds optimistically, "In time the people will learn, and develop.... The people will catch up with the wisdom that has been stored up for them" (333).

At first, William T.G. Morton in *Narkose* also has great faith in American democracy and science; and like Addams, he not only comments on American society but acts to make sure that justice is done in the case of someone he knows.[10] Morton believes in the future greatness of the United States because of the inventiveness and determination of its people, and he has a definite opinion about how his country should distinguish and assert itself in the mid-1800s. "Amerika muss Amerika werden," he says (28), meaning that Americans should stop allowing Europe to dictate their culture. The Monroe Doctrine is almost like sacred scripture to him and most of the medical students he knows: "Die Monroe-Bill! Denen, die sie gemacht, war sie ein Aktenstück. Uns ist sie Programm!" (29). His personal program includes taking time off from his dental practice and his experimentation to look for his wife's brother-in-law, who by hiding from the authorities is lessening his chances of being cleared of a murder charge.

Fritz Wieser in *Die japanische Pest* is another medical researcher who keeps abreast of current events and who takes action against a social evil.[11] The situation in this novel is unique, however: the central character has great opportunity to inform himself and discuss his observations, and the perspective of the narration is global rather than local.

Wieser has, first of all, an acute awareness of economic injustices in his homeland. He knows what it is to belong to the masses of hard-working people who are fleeced, as he says, for the benefit of the few millionaires (25). He is all but certain that as a researcher in Germany in 1922, he will not be able to earn a decent living for his family; and he has had enough of the "Sklavenfron des Kassenarztes" (6). Although the extremely well-paying temporary research position offered by the Japanese government will apparently solve his problems, Wieser is resentful of the fact that his native land does not provide financial security for most doctors and medical researchers and their families.

His social awareness is not limited to the economic plight of his own class in his own country, however. During his long luxury cruise to the Orient, Wieser is a model gentleman doctor and scientist, conversing philosophically with wealthy people of other countries and expressing an informed opinion about almost any topic that is introduced. Though the narrator says that Wieser is no lover of political discussions (27), the protagonist seems particularly interested in the effects of the national characters of various peoples on the world situation of his day.

Even later, when Wieser is absorbed in bacteriological research on a tiny Pacific island, his interest in "the big picture" is not diminished. His daily schedule, set by his employer, includes time for maintaining contact with the outside world by reading newspapers and, of course, by corresponding with his wife.

But Wieser is not one to be content with analyzing the world situation while sitting in comfort and security. He has accepted his present job partly because of his feeling that he must help save humankind from a dark cloud of untold destruction rising in the East and threatening to spread over the rest of the civilized world (12). His intuition proves accurate. When he discovers the plan of Japan's military to use an extremely virulent new form of plague to annihilate or subdue the populations of all other countries, he does his best to reach the American mainland in order to warn the Western nations. Unfortunately, he is recaptured by his Japanese "hosts" and executed by a firing squad.

Such a strong sense of duty to the world and specifically to the fatherland is evident in Robert Koch, as depicted in *Helfer der Menschheit*, even though he is at times oblivious to almost everything except his laboratory work.[12] As a young man, Koch idolizes Bismarck and puts his nationalistic feelings into action by serving as an army doctor at the front in the Franco-Prussian War. As a researcher much later, Koch is proud to serve his country again. With two assistants and a chemist, he travels to Egypt to represent Germany in what becomes a sort of contest with France to discover a cure for cholera. Although Koch is there primarily in the interests of science and medicine, he is aware that national honor is at stake: "Ob im Dienste der Menschheit oder nicht, zuerst galt es die Ehre jeder Nation!" (268). Similarly, Koch's later disease-fighting missions to foreign lands show not only his sense of medical and scientific duty to all of humanity but also his willingness to serve his government. His successes bring honor to Germany and make its colonization efforts in Africa safer.

Koch's expeditions, though they would seem well suited to satisfy his strong but long-suppressed desire to travel to faraway places, allow him almost no time for sightseeing. But as Koch shows during his long stay in India, whose ancient temples and exotic attractions he never gets to see, his sense of duty and his love for his work make him willing to forego such pleasure. The narrator says of this example of his hero's sacrifice, "Das Werk war stärker gewesen als die Sehnsucht seines Herzens" (296).

Martin Bertram makes greater concessions to culture and recreation than Koch does, but like the hero of *Helfer der Menschheit*, he has a great love for and sense of duty to the fatherland.[13] Like Josef Zeppichmann and Fritz Wieser, Bertram has firsthand knowledge of the economic injustice done to a particular group; but more like Richard Cameron, Alex Addams, and William T.G. Morton, he takes action on behalf of others to right a wrong. All in all, then, as medical researchers of fiction go, he has well-balanced interests.

Bertram feels that even in his private research, he is working for the honor of his country. He knows that if he can become the first to perfect an injectable general anesthetic, he will be adding to the glory of German science while securing his personal future. In the meantime, he censures what he thinks will discredit German science in the eyes of the world: he and his friend Wendemuth feel that the morbid curiosity of a colleague who plans an experiment with a human head separated from a corpse is "der deutschen Wissenschaft nicht würdig" (364).[14] Later, after Martin's success, his friend Wendemuth remarks that each ampule of Martin's anesthetic sold around the world will be a commendation for Germany (473). And in a spontaneous round of toasts at their victory celebration, Martin and his friends drink to the fatherland.

As indicated, Bertram also has other areas of interest besides medical science and the honor of his country. Despite the demands of his experimentation on the way to success, Martin does on occasion take time to mingle with the leisure class and to hike, ski, swim, dance, and play tennis. His participation in sports, especially hiking and skiing, is mentally as well as physically rewarding. After outings in the mountains, he is able to resume his work with more vigor and better concentration. His contact with the leisure class, however, is less beneficial. It reminds him of his usual lack of freedom and his great poverty in the last phase of his research project. On the other hand, this contact also makes him more determined to reach his research goal so that he can achieve financial independence.

Like Fritz Wieser, Bertram experiences both sides of the inequities of Germany's serious economic situation after World War I. At the beginning of the novel, he is the victim of a cutback at the hospital where he has been an orderly and a nurse. After several unsuccessful attempts to secure another such job, he impersonates a doctor in order to obtain a secure position in a distant city. Hired sight unseen, Bertram becomes a staff physician in a county hospital. At about the same time, he realizes a large profit from an investment and so becomes a man of means. Unfortunately, financing his research project takes almost all of his salary; and later, in an unpaid appointment at a state-run research institute, Bertram spends all of his savings. He then becomes personally acquainted with desperate poverty.

Bertram's own financial situation is not the only one which concerns him. He sees many people around him suffering because of economic injustice, and like some of his counterparts in other novels, he does what he can to remedy the situation. Acting specifically on behalf of his best friend, whose scientific brilliance goes unrewarded, Martin brings the plight of all the impoverished researchers to the attention of a wealthy and well-insulated co-director of the institute. He also informs that famous surgeon of the perpetual hunger of most medical students and newly graduated doctors without positions.

Like Martin Bertram and also like Richard Cameron, Martin Arrowsmith can be considered a spokesman for a particular type of social justice; however, his thinking runs opposite to that of most reformers.[15] Arrowsmith's cause is the right of the individual to work in peace without assuming any responsibility for others' welfare. He says, "Most people above the grade of hog do so much chasing around after a lot of vague philanthropy that they never get anything done" (292-293). He sides with the very few people who "have the courage to be decently selfish" and "demand the right to work" (293). At the end of the novel, he takes his ideal of the unencumbered worker to its logical conclusion when he joins fellow researcher Terry Wickett in a live-in laboratory in the middle of the wilderness.

Not all of Arrowsmith's actions, however, are consistent with his words. This fact makes him at once more realistic and sympathetic than he might otherwise be. After Martin says, "Nothing takes so much courage as to keep hard and clear-headed," the narrator interjects, "And he hadn't even that courage" (293). There are two people, Martin's wife Leora and his mentor Max Gottlieb, "whose unhappiness could always pierce him," at least until a chance discovery precipitates him into a monomaniacal burst of research activity (293).

Arrowsmith's involvement with research also keeps him unaware of important happenings in the world, even those which may affect the welfare of his country. Indicating the extent of Martin's ignorance of current events, the narrator also hints at a skeptical attitude toward international politics: "He was so absorbed in staphylolysin and in calculus that he did not realize the world was about to be made safe for democracy. He was a little dazed when America entered the war" (288).

Although Martin's feeling for his homeland never changes, it is from the beginning a different sort from that of most people around him. Expected to be an enthusiastic, active supporter of the United States' military effort during World War I, Martin says, "I want to be patriotic, but my patriotism is chasing antitoxins, doing my job, not wearing a particular kind of pants and a particular set of ideas about the Germans" (289). The narrator observes, "The war was to him chiefly another interruption to his work" (288). Not feeling the need to make a show of his love for his homeland, Martin soon becomes uncomfortable in the military uniform that he and the other civilian doctors at the research institute are asked to wear.

Martin has a similar experience with another type of "uniform"— the attitude required for moving in high society. For a while and to an extent, he learns to fit in with the rich and leisurely and takes part in their pastimes. He attends enough formal dinner parties to develop a tolerance for the company of "well-dressed nonentities" (407) and other people whom he does not like. At first he enjoys "the dramatic game of making Nice People accept him," but then he becomes "disturbed by reason" (407). To please his second wife Joyce, he plays at tennis and golf and other games. But just like Martin Bertram, he comes to the conclusion that his research work does not allow him to waste time on the recreation that some of his rich acquaintances take so seriously. He then reacts very negatively when Joyce chides him for not being one of the "big men who can do big work, and still stop and play" (420).

On occasion during the main part of the novel, Martin does give in to his need for therapeutic outdoor recreation and contact with nature, chiefly through hiking but also through swimming and canoeing, camping and picnicking. When he hikes, he does so in earnest, as when Leora takes him on a five-day walk on Cape Cod and when he goes on a solitary and rugged four-day outing in the hills of Vermont to combat nervous tension and insomnia. And after Martin takes up residence in Terry Wickett's cabin, outdoor exercise becomes a very regular part of his life.

Until this last phase of Martin's career, becoming cultured is another recurrent pursuit, the type of self-improvement changing as his commitment to research increases. As a country doctor, he has the time and the desire to fill in some of the great gaps in his general education. He reads European history and novels by Henry James and Joseph Conrad, meanwhile trying to improve his vocabulary and raise the level of his conversation. While working for a posh clinic in Chicago, he discovers "the world of book-shops and print-shops and theaters and concerts" (260). After becoming a salaried researcher, however, he "broadens" himself primarily with knowledge which relates to his job. He works much more diligently to reduce his deficiencies in mathematics and chemistry than to educate himself in the humanities and the social graces. He learns some German and French for the purpose of reading medical journals published in those languages.

Not all of Martin's leisure-time activities are intellectually enriching or physically beneficial, of course. In the novel there is mention of enjoyable but not particularly good movies, poker games, drinking bouts, and an intimate "bawdy" party (315) among other things. However, there is less and less of this type of recreation as Martin's career advances.

Ignaz Philipp Semmelweis, the central character of *The Cry and the Covenant* and *Retter der Mütter*, also has—for a time—a fairly wide range of outside interests.[16] His diversions and non-professional concerns are, as one would expect, limited by his commitment to ending childbed fever; and they are finally given up. However, with the exception of his short-lived political activism, these activities actually further his medical-scientific career.

Semmelweis, a proud and loyal Hungarian provincial, makes his revolutionary pathological discovery in Vienna and tries to gain general acceptance of it at a time of great suppression and unrest in the Austro-Hungarian Empire. Although he has little time and opportunity for active political involvement, Semmelweis is emotionally committed to the people's demands for basic freedoms and to Hungary's struggle for independence in the late 1840s. His activism, though limited, is picturesque. Twice he marches with students and professors of the University of Vienna to demand proper representation in government. For one of the marches, he dons a Hungarian military uniform and the golden sash of the revolution. Though he rarely even leaves his hospital ward during the ensuing riots, his Hungarian national costume becomes a regular feature there. But when asked to return to Hungary to fight for its freedom, he answers that he is needed in Vienna to fight for his doctrine of antisepsis.

Because Semmelweis feels that he must maintain an almost constant vigil to keep childbed fever from spreading in his ward at the Vienna General Hospital, he has time for virtually nothing else. His colleague and friend Hebra tells him to "play a little" so as not to become "like a piano with one key," but Semmelweis replies that until his doctrine is accepted, he cannot afford to lose a single patient (273).

It is only after his personal crusade has reached a complete dead end in Vienna (and after Hungary's revolution has failed) that Semmelweis returns to his homeland and learns how to play. At his friend Markussovsky's urging to "get a few social graces" (346) in order to build up a private practice in obstetrics and gynecology, Semmelweis conscientiously indulges in the amusements of high society. With Markussovsky's financial support, he takes up horseback riding, dancing, dining in good restaurants, and attending the theater.

Like other main characters, however, Semmelweis comes to realize that he can scarcely afford time for entertainment or even for cultural enrichment. Just when he is becoming a fairly well-rounded socialite, he begins to feel guilty about "this new life" (355) because he is not doing enough to fight puerperal fever. He says, "I wake up nights, my heart pounding. I've dreamed that I've found a cure and they won't accept it. I'm wet with sweat. I shudder from my nightmare. I rub my eyes. I'm awake—and it's true" (355).

Soon enough, almost all of Semmelweis' leisure activities and outside interests have become things of the past. He lectures at the University of Pesth, runs a clinic and a hospital ward, and, to make good on his vow to do everything possible to defeat childbed fever, undertakes the writing of a scientific treatise on the effectiveness of his basic sanitary measures. To provide ongoing clinical proof of his doctrine, he stalks his maternity ward day and night to make sure that strict sanitary procedure is always followed. Semmelweis finally becomes a monomaniac, losing his sanity to his cause.

The cases above suggest that medical researchers, like other people, sooner or later give in to the need for diversion from their occupational pursuits, even though extraprofessional interests may later be dropped.

Most of the main characters, when not in the most intense phase of research, have at least one important social or cultural concern in addition to recreation. Several of the doctor-scientists take direct action for a specific social or political cause. Understandably, however, most of them do not have either the opportunity or the desire to become especially well-rounded; and when their research work is at its peak, they become very one-sided indeed.

With regard to the world outside the central characters' professional sphere, another important, though obvious, observation should be made. Regardless of individual concerns or non-concerns in the realm of economics, politics, and culture, all of the chief characters find their research work to be their best way of affecting human affairs. Of course, most never find themselves in Fritz Wieser's situation—being the only person who can save most of the world's population from imminent annihilation. Neither are the majority of them ever as willing as Martin Arrowsmith to disclaim all non-professional responsibility for their fellow human beings. They are well inside the two extremes, enriching humanity primarily by doing their work (but sometimes making contributions in other areas) and occasionally seeking enrichment and refreshment in humankind's general affairs.

Chapter Six
Beliefs About the Ultimate Authority

Since a thorough character study ought to include its subject's basic metaphysical beliefs, the protagonists' ideas about the governing force of the universe will now be examined. In light of the rise of materialism in the last two centuries, one might expect all of the fictional medical researchers to be atheists who think that science can ultimately explain everything and that the human mind is therefore the highest authority. However, as a group these doctor-scientists, like people in virtually any profession, are divided in their beliefs on this subject. In medical research novels, the highest power is assigned in turn to the human mind, nature, fate, and various conceptions of God. Approximately a third of the central characters firmly believe that the laws of nature presuppose a Creator. On the other hand, some of the main characters who believe in a force which predetermines and/or actively directs human events are not convinced that it is personal or generally benevolent. Most of the group does, however, find the idea of some such force either very appealing or at least interesting in a theoretical way.

Unfortunately, it is not possible in every case to determine the chief character's actual beliefs in these matters. Such terms as *nature, fate,* and *God* sometimes appear to be used as rhetorical conventions rather than definite philosophical concepts.[1]

In any case, the following discussion, by means of the many examples presented, will reveal that the central characters' opinions on this subject are not affected greatly by their experiences in medical research. Rather, their commitment to medical science tends to reinforce the ideas which they already hold, although it limits their time for any active concern with metaphysics. As one might expect, the beliefs of parents or other role models exert a strong influence on many of the medical researchers.

Although Georg Letham's counterparts are seldom shown seriously questioning their own metaphysical suppositions, the chief character and narrator of *Georg Letham, Arzt und Mörder* does struggle with the concepts of fate, God, and nature.[2] He sometimes suspects that some supernatural force may be shaping his life and determining events in general. He notes that certain experiences seem designed to settle scores and teach him lessons. He often mentions *Schicksal* and nature and at least considers the existence of God. While maintaining that his upbringing has made him too cynical to believe in any supernaturally imposed meaning and order to the world (24), Letham says that he envies people who believe in God and miracles.

Because he is a pathologist as well as a cynic, Letham sees plenty of examples of "tiefe und wahrhaft schauerliche, katastrophale Unordnung und Sinnlosigkeit der Natur und der Umwelt" (7). Although as a scientist he must believe in some system of natural laws, he is more forcibly struck by those things in nature that appear senseless—"Schmerz, Leid der Seele, Qual des Körpers in unvorstellbarem Ausmass, und dabei idiotische Kraft- und Materialvergeudung der Natur in dieser wohlgeordnetsten aller Welten" (7). Letham sees one indication of nature's wastefulness and lack of consistent purpose in the fact that strong, young people are more likely to contract yellow fever than old, weak ones. Making this observation, he grumbles, "Ewiger Irrsinn der Natur, die sich mit den Worten 'gütig' und 'liebevolle Mutter' schmeicheln lässt, die alte geschminkte Dirne" (226).

Letham feels that as an objective thinking man, he is obliged to see and comprehend the dark side of existence. As a scientist, he cannot enjoy the luxury of accentuating the positive or of simply ignoring the distasteful things of life. Rather, he is "gezwungen, dies alles wissend und begreifend mitansehen zu müssen" (8).

Of course, Letham must not only be part of the select audience viewing the drama of life with understanding; he must also accept a part in the play. At times he mentions playing the role fate has written for him.

Curiously, Letham's attitude toward fate is not a strictly scientific attitude toward the turn of events. Instead, he reacts to fate as to a stern but sometimes encouraging person of authority. He has a habit of calling an unusual happening at a significant moment "ein Wink des Schicksals" (319, 364, 485), and at times he speculates about omens. Twice he offers a pact to fate, as a religious person might make a conditional promise to God. Once Letham makes it seem that he has some say in the matter of fate: in the type of situation in which other people might speak of letting nature take its course, he says that he has decided not to interfere with fate (287). He also expresses the idea that his suffering or self-denial can mitigate his guilt, improve him, and even help balance accounts with fate.

Thus, Letham seems to believe, at least temporarily, in something like karma. The death of the young Portuguese girl with whom he has fallen in love brings·him to the conclusion that he is paying in kind for his earlier misdeeds. He says, "Ich begriff den Zusammenhang zwischen dem früheren und dem späteren" (287). When certain details from his past are repeated in the present, Letham uses the expression

"Ironie des Schicksals" (380, 426) or "...wie kehrt doch alles wieder in diesem kurzen Leben" (287, 294).

Many times, however, a bad experience causes Letham to think of fate as blundering, blind, unfair, or cruel. At one critical juncture, he asks himself, "Aber kann ich an ein *sinnvolles* Schicksal glauben, kann ich es, der ich doch vom ersten Augenblick die Sinnlosigkeit und stupide Grausamkeit des Weltenlaufes habe erkennen müssen!" (270). He decries the injustice in the fact that certain good people close to him have died of yellow fever and certain bad people of his acquaintance have recovered from it. He says bitterly that fate has betrayed him twice (365). In another situation, he says, "Ich schob alle Schuld den Verhältnissen, der ungeschickten oder böswilligen Hand des Schicksals zu" and asks rhetorically if one must regard the world and oneself as "Objekte eines grausigen, unmenschlichen, zynischen Humors" (469-470). At his emotional low point, he refers to himself as a wretched "Schöpfung eines liederlich experimentierenden Schicksals" (372).

Letham expresses the hopeless wish that he could at least believe in a supersensible order in the world (8), and he really seems to need such a higher authority—some agency, mythical or real, on which to blame the wretchedness he has seen and felt. As shown, he rails against nature and fate; he also makes sarcastic references to God. For example, he calls yellow fever, typhus, cancer, tuberculosis and other horrible diseases "herrliche Erfindungen Gottes" (238). Finding out that he will be the first of the newly arrived prisoners to be exposed to yellow fever, he says with irony, "Gott verlässt die Seinen nicht" (226). Letham conjectures that humanity may actually be quite unimportant to the higher power (if the latter exists):

Vielleicht bedeuten wir der höheren Gewalt über uns (ich kann nicht an sie glauben und doch tritt sie mir manchmal in meinen Gedankenkreis) nicht mehr und nicht weniger als unsereinem Katzen oder Hunde, Ratten, Meerschweinchen, Affen, Pferde und selbst— Wanzen und Läuse. (25)

He also points out with some bitterness that fate or nature or God can do with impunity what is considered the worst crime a human being can commit: "Morden darf nur ungestraft das Schicksal" (237-238); "Morden soll die erbarmungslose Natur oder Gott" (288).

As the last two quotations show, Letham essentially equates fate, nature, and God—that is, a tentative concept of a God with negative capabilities, since he cannot believe in a benevolent deity. This interchangeability of concepts can be seen again in the words with which Letham begins another statement about fate: "Das Schicksal (nennt es Gott oder Teufel oder Natur—das gleiche bleibt es!)..." (483).

Although he wishes that he could believe in a benign supreme authority and envies two co-workers their comforting religious faith, Letham cannot resolve his own spiritual conflict: "Ich glaubte nicht an Gott. Ich konnte keine übernatürliche Sinngebung in der Welt anerkennen. Gerne hätte ich es gewollt. Möglich war es nicht" (24). He can neither bring himself to spiritual belief nor live without the need for it, he says (24). Letham does not, however, pray to God, even when very close to death. He illuminates further the nature of his dilemma:

Könnte ich mich vor dem "Wunderwerk der Schöpfung Gottes" in kritikloser Anbetung beugen! Beten! Könnte ich endlich der logischen Verzweiflung Herr werden, die mich entwurzelt, mich aber auch klar gemacht, die mich gelähmt, aber auch geschützt und beschirmt hat seit den entscheidenden Versuchen meines Vaters an mir als Kind! (94)

Letham says that because of his father's psychological experiments on him as a child, he has been rendered incapable of reconciling faith in divine order and justice with an honest view of existence. He describes at some length the planting of the seeds of doubt that grew into tough cynicism. His father encouraged him to go to church and to pray faithfully yet supplied him all the while with overwhelming evidence of the world's basic senselessness and brutality. Letham's formal scientific training and his own observations then naturally reinforced his father's skillful teaching.

Oddly enough, however, when Letham poses the key question, "Kann man Wissenschaft trotz allem mit positivem Glauben verbinden?" (128), he himself answers in the affirmative. He cites Louis Pasteur as "ein das ganze medizinische Gebäude seiner Zeit erschütternder und grandios neu aufbauender Forscher—und zugleich ein frommer Katholik" (128). Likewise, Letham's colleague Walter is not only an excellent scientist but "Ein frommer Mensch, der der Religion seiner Jugendjahre treu geblieben war und ihr bis ans Ende treu bleiben musste" (303).

Letham himself seems close to believing at times but really only flirts with religious faith. Any statement of his which may sound religious is just a manner of speech, as when he remarks, ". . . ich dankte meinem Schöpfer (wenn ich diese Phrase anwenden darf) oft" (400). When anyone important to him is dying and medical science can do no more, Letham hopes for a miracle but never really expects one. Of one such instance he says, "Statt der Wissenschaft nahm ich, nicht der erste und nicht der letzte, zu dem Kinderglauben meine Zuflucht" (279). Quite late in the novel, however, he asks doubtfully, ". . . gibt es Wunder? Gibt es einen Himmel?" (481). Moreover, a few pages earlier, the narrator Letham is unabashed in saying, ". . . ich schwöre es bei dem Heiligsten, was es für einen Menschen meiner Art geben kann, ich schwöre es bei mir selbst" (478).

This last quotation really marks the furthest extent of Georg Letham's thinking about metaphysical matters. Incapable of belief in the supernatural (or so he says) and unconvinced of a sensible order in nature, he can see nothing more worthy than his scientific mind. Crippled by his father's teaching and also preoccupied with his research work, Letham makes only a foreshortened and prejudiced spiritual quest.

He does, however, acknowledge one power higher than his own. He recognizes nature's imperviousness to human will: "Was vermag Menschenwille? Er zwingt die Natur nicht auf die Knie" (385-386). And as already stated, his observations as a medical scientist make him despair of human ability even to superimpose an order on nature. In terms of his own life, Letham must continually bow to the will of fate, which in the final analysis seems to be the same thing as nature—if indeed *fate* means anything more to him than a convenient literary device for dealing with the unexplainable.

The outcome of Richard Cameron's much shorter spiritual quest is told in less than a page in *The Undaunted*. With some time on his hands and a burden on his conscience, Cameron finds himself confronted with "the agonizing question of adolescence: What is it all about? What is life for?" (292). He wonders if, by having concentrated his energies on medical research for so many years, he has neglected some higher purpose. Science, after all, is "concerned with *How*, not *Why*" (292) and so cannot provide an answer to his question about life. Nevertheless, Cameron's venture into metaphysics is half-hearted and easily summarized: "Religion told him nothing of either *How* or *Why* that he could accept. Philosophy repelled him" (292). As mentioned in another context, Cameron decides to "leave the problems of the universe" to people who enjoy pondering such matters and who are intellectually better suited to do so (292).

Alex Addams does not concede to issues of cosmic import a complexity beyond his grasp; but since he as an adult has looked to no higher power than that of the scientific mind, he has spent little time considering the possibility that something else may be the final authority in the universe.[3] While acknowledging and respecting great powers in nature, he remains quite confident that science is steadily gaining control over it. He gives no credence—indeed, no thought at all—to the concept of fate as a real force. Addams does, however, participate in some stimulating discussions of theist religion, primarily because the author Irving Fineman was very interested in exploring the subject of belief in the Judeo-Christian God.

Addams appears to have decided long ago against the possibility of a rational religion. He tells his father:

I cannot now remember that I have ever had any faith in divinity expressible in prayer and praise; only a fearful sense of powers in the universe outside my circumscribed sight. I must have been born agnostic; and as soon as I had grown enough to look over the edges of that fence of authority you and my childhood teachers had set up around me, the whole concept of deist [theist] religion became unimportant if not ridiculous to me. (289-290)

On the other hand, he indicates elsewhere that no scientist would refuse to believe in an active God if only someone "could once prove God an unknown quantity really pertinent to his equations" (352).

In the meantime, the younger Addams finds "repugnant" the idea of a scientist's turning to the Church for "authoritative solutions of all problems outside the field of his work" (158). He sees only disharmony in the mentality of his colleague Francis MacBride, a devout Catholic. Addams maintains that while scientists "climb painfully, patiently, but securely tied by the age-long chain of logic," the religious "fly by a leap through the dark" to their concept of God as First Cause (11). Yet in all metaphysical matters, he himself has a carefully guarded bias: "He preferred even ignorant avoidance of such problems. It was better, certainly for a scientist, to be agnostic, than blindly faithful where he couldn't work the matter out for himself" (158).

Religious people, Addams thinks, have a very unscientific attitude toward nature, not to mention other things. However, his attitude here seems inconsistent with the above. He suggests that people were nearer to science "when they had magic" than after they "got gods" and "began to invoke a capricious god for their need" (11). He thinks it curious that "the religious ask for neither knowledge of nature nor power over it" (11); when people resorted to magic, at least they "presumed a consistent nature over which they superstitiously attempted to obtain power" (11). Understandably, a regular and predictable nature subject to human control appeals to the scientist's love of order and power whereas an untamable and unpredictable God does not.

Particularly unpalatable to Addams is organized religion's combining earthly authority with heavenly-mindedness. He objects to what he sees as the Church's use of intimidation: "But men who live in fear, of God and of death, are stultified; they can have no grandeur" (353). He remarks to his Catholic colleague, "The prospect of an ultimate society of submissive slaves and powerful if paternal rulers, whether priests or politicians, is abhorrent to me" (353). And even if the Church can somehow avoid being corrupted by its power, Addams feels, its energies will always be misdirected because "if its eyes are fixed on another world, it escapes the living reality, denies its possible perfection" (354).

However, Addams' turning to science can also be seen as an attempt to escape the living reality, at least the disquieting parts. Symbolically, he is shown fleeing from spirituality and commercialism (and perhaps the mainstream of humanity?) as he takes refuge in his laboratory. After an intense conversation in which Addams is confronted with the nagging questions, "...what have you done for the spirits of men with all your ungodly proofs; how is it in your own heart; are you secure?" and "Can you make a sustaining creed out of your scientific passion?" (352-353), the narrator says, "Addams, as if still in flight, turned from the traffic-filled square between the Cathedral and the [Radio] Tower and entered the quiet foyer of the Foundation" (354-355).

Addams' father, a doctor who has not become a researcher, presents additional religious challenges to science. A New England Protestant, the elder Addams tells his son,

Still, as you see, I pray, I speak of God. I cannot relinquish God, the lawful Creator, who provides human life with that ethical order, that dignity of form and intention without which all life is an anarchy. I cannot give up the God who remains for me the repository for those mysteries in nature, those seemingly capricious events whose lawful consistency men have not yet grasped. (290)

Although Addams' father does not "live in fear of punishment or expectation of reward after death" (290), he asserts, "We suffer to the extent that we do not, either in willfulness or ignorance [sic], order our lives according to cosmic law"; and he notes that humanity is still, despite science's best efforts, "a long way from knowing all that law" (290). "So," the elder Addams advises, "we had better hold for a while to God, for coherence, for defense against the disintegration which is in the air" (291).

The religious beliefs of the wise, dignified, and sympathetic Joshua Addams, though not necessarily intended to convince the reader, are at least fairly presented—in contrast to the statements of Francis MacBride, whose mannerisms show him to be prim, old-fashioned, repressed, and extreme. Thus, Fineman lends credibility to a viewpoint opposing his protagonist's and yet censures fanaticism.

The younger Addams accepts the "irreconcilable divergence" of his and his father's outlooks (291), attributing the elder's religious faith to that generation's lack of freedom. The narrator says, "His father's generation, he saw now, had never been free; it had been unlicensed; and it had divided itself between virtuous, self-restraining orthodoxy and sinful unscrupulousness" (291). The younger Addams feels "far removed now from either, emancipated from all of it" (291).

He does not, like Georg Letham, rue his inability to believe in God, yet he does feel a "pang of regret" about the passing of "those times when sons naturally, wholeheartedly, without the shadow of doubt or rebellion, took over the vision and philosophy of their fathers" (291-292). There was peace and security in that arrangement, he thinks.

Martin Arrowsmith is another protagonist who cannot reconcile science and a belief in the supernatural and has no wish to do so.[4] He entertains no notions about an irresistible fate and rejects the concepts of God and the human soul. The power which concerns him is that of his intelligence and his will. The workings of Martin's scientific mind and of his determination are shown against the backdrop of the narrator's occasional hints that nature will have the final say in this world.

From Martin's point of view, any religious doctrine is mere speculation since it is unprovable by scientific method. His mentor, Max Gottlieb, has contempt for "the preachers who talk their fables" (267), and Martin comes to feel the same way. When Martin starts medical school, he has but a "feeble belief in man's divinity and immortality" (16), and his education in medicine and related sciences causes him to lose even that. He reveres the human body not as the handiwork of the Creator but as a fascinating, complex, and beautiful machine; he has yet to discover a soul among the organs (16-17). Neither the laws of nature nor unexplainable phenomena convince him of the existence of a divine plan. He regards all spirituality as anti-scientific wishful thinking.

Besides, by immersing himself in medical research, Martin can effectively avoid problems in metaphysics. He develops a distrust of the motives of people who are after the "secret of life" and convinces himself "that there is no Truth but only many truths; that Truth is not a colored bird to be chased among the rocks and captured by its tail, but a skeptical attitude toward life" (260).

Despite Martin's feelings about spirituality and absolute truth, his devotion to science is not terribly unlike religious zeal. Throughout the novel, Sinclair Lewis plays on this irony and, like Christian apologists, shows a fondness for paradoxes. "Like all ardent agnostics, Martin was a religious man," says the narrator, explaining that the young Arrowsmith must always have a passionate belief in some idea and some person (165). Martin's devotion to successive heroes of medical science is, in fact, directly compared to religious fanaticism. At one point, the narrator says that Martin "preached to himself, as Max Gottlieb had once preached to him, the loyalty of dissent, the faith of being very doubtful, the gospel of not bawling gospels" (219). Elsewhere, Martin tells his fraternity brothers that Gottlieb's mere presence in a laboratory is a prayer (31), and Gottlieb himself insists that "the scientist is intensely religious—he is so religious that he will not accept quarter-truths, because they are an insult to his faith" (267). Martin, in his "prayer of the scientist," prays, "God give me strength not to trust to God!" (269).

The employment of paradox and irony can also become blasphemous, from a Judeo-Christian point of view, as when Gottlieb, whose very name is ironic, says to Martin, "May Koch bless you!" (268) or when Martin kneels beside his bed and prays to his absent wife Leora (370).

Lewis' irreverence and love of satire are nowhere more evident than in his portrayal of the Reverend Ira Hinkley. Hinkley, an overbearing, bothersome fraternity brother of Martin's, becomes a missionary doctor and serves on the same island where Martin conducts his great plague experiment. Lewis' narrator describes Hinkley as a huge, strong man who can bellow like a steer (16). "He was a bright and happy Christian," he adds, "a romping optimist who laughed away sin and doubt, a joyful Puritan who with annoying virility preached the doctrine of his tiny sect" (16). Hearing that Hinkley can hardly wait to "heal the bodies and comfort the souls of countless lost unhappy folks" (17), Martin pities the poor heathen who will be bullied into submission (18). When Martin asks if Hinkley honestly believes "that junk" about the immortal soul, the latter retorts, "You think you've got a lot of these fancy Modern Doubts. You haven't—you've only got indigestion. What you need is exercise and faith" (17). Years later, Hinkley tries to prevent Martin's plague experiment by discrediting Martin as a doctor and a scientist. He tells the islanders that the plague is the wrath of God come upon them, and he calls Gottlieb and Arrowsmith "liars and fools" and "scorners of righteousness" (361-362). Four days after making these remarks, Hinkley himself dies of the plague, falling right beside his pulpit.

The epidemic is, in effect, a symbol of nature's indifference to all of humanity's beliefs and acquired powers. The plague claims the lives of Leora, the great love of Martin's life, and Gustaf Sondelius, the great fighter of contagions. Furthermore, as pointed out earlier, serious questions arise concerning the actual effectiveness of Martin's vaccine in stopping the epidemic. It should also be remembered that Max Gottlieb, in his early work, expressed doubts about the ultimate good of immunization in general.

Martin himself, however, never concedes that nature will inevitably have the upper hand. His only comment about nature as a personified force, though much like Georg Letham's observations, lacks their earnestness: "He denounced Nature for her way of tricking human beings, by every gay device of moonlight and white limbs and reaching loneliness, into having babies, then making birth as cruel and clumsy and wasteful as she could" (167).

Like the narrators of *Doctor Addams* and *Arrowsmith*, the narrator of *Die japanische Pest* is much more interested in the subject of a higher order than is the main character.[5] Like Martin Arrowsmith and Alex Addams, Fritz Wieser sees no reason to believe in God. And although he once speaks metaphorically about submitting to the will of fate, he simply means that there is no point in worrying about what might have been: "Es bleibt da wohl nichts übrig, als Ergebung in den Willen des Geschickes, das es so und nicht anders über die Menschheit verhängte" (52). He is also quick to point out that a person is responsible for his or her own fate: "Im Anfang war die Tat" (53). Wieser is not sure who or what, other than the laws of nature, may be in control of the universe; but even at the point of death, he takes no active interest in finding out. He waives his right to talk with a priest before being executed by a Japanese firing squad. His scientific mind cannot believe anything that has not been proven, and his culture's God is no more real to him than other cultures' gods whose images he has seen in his travels.

Traditional Western concepts of life and fate are also challenged in this novel. Before Wieser leaves his homeland to work with the Japanese, an Indian fakir presents him and the reader with what becomes the central assertion of the novel, that one can live another life in a moment's time—a past life, a future life, or the life one *may* yet live by making certain choices of action instead of others (19). Although Wieser later meets several individuals who tell of having lived another life, he remains incredulous until he has experienced death and returned to life. Immediately after being shot to death by the firing squad, he finds himself in a familiar salon in Berlin, resuming his conversation with the fakir. From that point forward, he relives all of the experiences of that evening of about a year before. This time, however, he reacts differently at each juncture. Most importantly, he decides not to join the Japanese research project. He thereby alters his own fate, the fate of others around him, and in fact, the fate of the whole world.

It is not certain whether the author Ludwig Anton is trying to make an overall statement about life, the soul, and deity; but his unusual, entertaining, and thought-provoking novel seems to have certain didactic features. For example, the last words which Wieser hears before his execution are surely meant to sound prophetic: "Was wir Tod nennen, ist der Übergang zu einem andern, zum nächsten Leben. Man schreitet durchs Vergessen, aber man lebt weiter. Bis die Gottheit, des Träumens müde, eine andere Welt erschafft" (239). Anton's use of the non-specific term *die Gottheit* and his presentation of various religions and many gods with literally the same face would seem to indicate that he sees no important differences in the various concepts of God. And by showing that Wieser can, to an extent, determine his own fate and that of the entire world, Anton may well be suggesting that every individual has this kind of control and can, by his or her choices of action, affect everyone else's life.

In any case, Anton is clearly proposing that there is more to existence than can be proven by science; there is indeed a spiritual realm. The chief character, even before his enlightening experience, speaks of the bankruptcy of materialism (70). Although Wieser is contemptuous of spiritual "Aberglauben" and "Wahnideen," he blames materialism for the destruction of faith and morals, the upheaval of the social order, and the unleashing of World War I (70). Such turmoil, he says, has caused the general public to return to church and has driven the educated class into occultism, mysticism, and various other "Ismen" (70). Wieser explains: "Vor diesem Materialismus, der die alte uns vertraute Welt zerstört hat und nicht imstande ist, eine neue aufzubauen, in der wir uns wohnlich einrichten können, flieht die Menschheit" (70). As for spirituality, Wieser naturally has much more sympathy after he has experienced death and reanimation.

Alfried Kalsten in *Patrouille gegen den Tod* would agree with Wieser at least on the point that humanity seems to have spiritual needs.[6] Kalsten, witnessing on the one hand nature's great hostility and on the other hand a wide variety of religious rites and relics, understands dying people's need for a type of comfort that medical science cannot give them. When he himself is in a dangerous situation, he decides that anyone who has lost his or her religious beliefs is without a potentially important recourse. He remarks, "Schade, dass wir den braven Kinderglauben in der Zeiten Läufte verloren haben. Mann könnte ihn manchmal brauchen!" (193).

As in *Die japanische Pest*, there seems to be a very relativistic view of spiritual beliefs in *Patrouille*. All of the various final rites administered to victims of the *Kanda-Kanda-Seuche* are considered equally valid for the purpose of comforting the dying, and any comparative value judgment of the many religions seems to be discouraged.

One notable incident appears to support the conclusion that one religion serves as well as another, depending on where one happens to be. When Kalsten's travelling party becomes lost in the brush, the native Congolese guide, supposedly a Christian convert, prays to the image of a jungle god, explaining, "Ich guter Christ, von Weissen Vätern getauft. Ich brav in Loaluanda zur Messe gehen. Aber hier im Walde auch starker Gott; Tschigulla-Wuda ganz mächtig.... In Kinshasha, im Licht, wird wieder herrschen Jesus Christ" (192). Kalsten is impressed with the strength of his guide's conviction, and the lost travellers' rest stop by the idol allows them to discover a path back to civilization. The author may even be making a symbolic statement here, but the text allows for no certainty on this point.

The one deity of *Angela Koldewey* is a given rather than a remote possibility acceptable to only the childlike mind.[7] God is also of personal importance to the central character. As mentioned elsewhere in this study, Angela feels called by God, first to medical practice and then to medical research. She needs to feel in harmony with God, eternity, nature, and the world. At the end of her life, she is grateful to God for what she has been allowed to accomplish.

At times Angela's God seems more like Brahma than Jehovah, as when the narrator says that Angela feels a new bond developing between herself and the entity which is "Gott, Ewigkeit, Welt, alles" (106). By the end of the novel, however, this God has revealed a more definite personality and demonstrated direct involvement not only in humanity's fate in general but also in Angela Koldewey's in particular.

Even so, Angela has her time of despair and doubt. Right after she learns of her terminal illness, she loses her faith that the world is regulated by eternal laws; she begins to think that everything must be the product of blind coincidence (137). She permanently rejects a priest's assertion that the raison d'etre of the afflicted is to awaken love, selflessness, and the spirit of sacrifice in others, thereby becoming living songs of praise to God's glory (138). Angela believes in justification through personal achievement; and having become one of the afflicted herself, she feels that God has abandoned her after giving her false hopes of accomplishment.

She does, however, regain spiritual equilibrium when she discovers her true destiny and the way to fulfill it. Her God works all things out for good in the end, not only perpetuating life—at least for its predetermined length—but enriching life as well.

Martin Bertram also believes in a god, but not necessarily the God who directly determines the course of events.[8] For this reason, Bertram seems more like a deist than a Christian, although he comes from a long line of Lutheran ministers. While comforting a dying patient who seeks convincing answers about the afterlife, he says that true scientists have never denied the existence of God (234). In his daily life, however, he does little to counter the impiety and lack of belief of the times in which he lives. He is, as his assistant and friend Hans Hühnerdieb says, "nicht sehr stark im Glauben" (429). Indeed, when he talks about the workings of a higher power, he mentions fate rather than God.

Bertram is much more a man of action than of faith: celebrating the research triumph to which his friends have helped him, he remarks, "Aber die richtige Hilfe fällt nicht vom Himmel, man muss zu den Leuten halten, die zu einem passen, und dabei bleiben. Konsequent bleiben— das ist es" (475). Earlier, he has conceded that these all-important friendships are predetermined (430-431); but in this and similar connections, Bertram uses the term *Schicksal*, not *Gott*. He does not make pronouncements about God's workings and God's will except when he observes sarcastically, "Immer gewinnt der Stärkere, und immer ist der liebe Gott bei den stärksten Bataillonen" (51).

The author, on the other hand, seems more than casually interested in the subject of God. Many times (and usually at crisis points) in the course of Martin's experiment, Hans Hühnerdieb makes statements about his own faith. The childlike and pious Hühnerdieb, who is studying to become a missionary doctor, is, on the whole, meant to be taken seriously: he is courageous, hard-working, generous, and self-effacing. The narrator shows that Hühnerdieb derives real benefit from his religion, and the assistant's faith in Martin Bertram and Bertram's "gottgefälliges Werk" (429) is a big factor in the success of the project. If Hühnerdieb's more sectarian beliefs (such as vegetarianism) do not seem to have authorial sanction, it is not for any lack of sincerity, consistency, or humaneness on the character's part.

In Theo Malade's *Semmelweis, der Retter der Mütter*, there is some of the same kind of interplay among the agencies of nature, fate, God, and the human being that there is in *Georg Letham*.[9] Semmelweis and the narrator apparently conceive of nature in about the same way that Georg Letham does, frankly admitting its whimsical and sometimes very destructive side. Fate in *Retter der Mütter*, as in *Letham*, is sometimes seen as heavy-handed. There are, however, two major differences in the outlooks of the two novels' main characters. Semmelweis has much more faith in the effectiveness of human action, and though not a regular churchgoer, he believes in the Christian God who directs the courses of nature and human fate by intervening in history.

Of course, Semmelweis is not always pleased with his fate as it unfolds, nor is he constantly assured of God's good purposes: "Anfangs wehrte er sich wohl gegen das ihm aufgezwungene Geschick mit all' dem Aufbegehren, dessen sein wallendes Herz fähig war" (71). However, the more he understands God's plan for him, the less he resents and resists it: "Allmählich liess die innere Spannkraft nach. Was hatte die Quälerei, das ewige Ringen für einen Zweck?" (71). Indeed, Semmelweis considers his revolutionary medical discovery a holy trust and a gift from a benevolent God: "Ein gütiger Gott hatte ihm gegeben, eine ewige Wahrheit zu finden. So felsenfest war er von der Richtigkeit seiner Gedankengänge und Schlüsse überzeugt, dass er dies Endergebnis als heiliges Vermächtnis empfand" (32). As shown in another reaction, Semmelweis feels that fate in general and he in particular are being guided by God: "Das war ein lebendiges Zeichen, das ihm der Himmel schickte! Das bedeutete die Bestätigung der einzigen, urewigen Wahrheit seiner Lehre durch das Schicksal!" (100).

God's active grace is seen to shine through the bright side of nature and to overcome the dark side. Semmelweis exults in the supernatural revelation by means of which he has been called to free humanity from the "Dämon" that hinders it in fulfilling its highest duty, reproduction

(100-101). The two sides of nature and an indication of God's plan are seen again in the conclusion of the novel. The narrator remarks that nature, often very fickle in distributing its gifts, did not give Semmelweis all the qualities necessary for him to see antisepsis put into universal practice during his lifetime; but it did give him the deep compassion which motivated his research (124-125).

Human agency in fate is not by any means minimized by Malade or his hero. The narrator makes it clear at the end of the novel that Semmelweis' discovery was not the result of a lucky coincidence but was rather "die Frucht bewusster wissenschaftlicher Arbeit und felsenfester Überzeugung" (124). In other words, though God put Semmelweis in the proper situation to make certain observations, the medical scientist had to use his own brain and hands to accomplish the requisite research.

In *Helfer der Menschheit*, which is almost exclusively narration, it is very difficult to determine which of the ideas expressed are Robert Koch's and which are solely the narrator's.[10] However, the indications are that Koch is a God-fearing though not an actively religious man and that he does not conceive of nature or fate or the human being as independent forces. Reared in "Frömmigkeit und Rechtschaffenheit" (30), he evidently continues to believe in an omniscient, omnipotent, and omnipresent God. As a medical student, he makes each new discovery in nature with a sense of wonder and considers the human being God's most glorious creation (54). As a doctor, he takes his responsibilities very seriously, considering himself to be in partnership with God for the purpose of healing (67). As a highly creative and very determined researcher, he is called "ein ursprünglicher Mensch, in dessen Blutstrom die ewigen Quellen Gottes rauschen, der einen Hauch verspürte von der Urkraft des ersten Schöpfungstages" (111). Koch is said to be, like other great discoverers in all fields of endeavor, a mediator between the extrasensory and the sensory worlds; he and other pioneers bring humanity and the cosmos into accord (184). In Unger's novel, nothing is left to blind chance and an impersonal fate; the grace of God allows certain creative persons to direct humanity's course. The narrator speaks of the "grosse Gnade, schöpferisch tätig zu sein und durch unerhörte Taten das Schicksal der Menschheit in neue Bahnen zu lenken" (299).

In *Shannon's Way* the protagonist's very strong belief in the God of Christianity is quite obvious.[11] In fact, of all of the chief characters, Robert Shannon adheres most conscientiously to organized religion. Unfortunately, it cannot be said that he confirms his faith by answering scientific challenges to it. He generally ignores the objections and clings to his religion because of his upbringing and tradition—in short, because it feels right. He describes himself as "a Catholic, who had strayed occasionally into the less dark corridors of scepticism, but who still, at heart, clung to his first belief" (45). Despite the "irregularity" of his life as a medical researcher and the "damaging conflicts" of his mind, Shannon attends Mass occasionally because of what he calls "the irrevocable instinct in my bones" (70). The frequent needling of a co-worker who attempts to "put nails in the coffin" of Shannon's religious faith with "metaphysical expositions" (27) serves only to make him unapologetic about it. To the taunt, "I thought you were a scientist. You can't reconcile Genesis and the mutation of species," Shannon replies, "I don't try to. The one is a sordid fact...the other a romantic mystery" (29). Nor does he try to provide logical proof of the other tenets of his religion. He meets the skeptic's objections with the statement, "All the same, there's something that I can't ever get away from...against reason if you like.... I hope you don't wish me to say that I regret it" (29).

For a loyal Catholic, however, Shannon has a curious attitude toward fate. Extremely self-sufficient, he feels that he must "take issue with authority and fate" (18), as if the course of his life had nothing to do with God. Throughout most of the novel, he is engaged in an unsuccessful attempt to chart his own course. Although early in the novel he mentions making an occasional "act of reparation" and "promise of amendment" in church (70), Shannon generally seems to want no external guidance of his life.

When he tells someone, "I must confess that my biological work has somewhat restricted my opportunities for churchgoing" (45), Shannon is euphemizing his normal inattention to spiritual matters. His religious faith is not something he lives but something he carefully preserves, like an old family heirloom usually kept out of sight. Contemplating it from time to time brings him comfort, and guarding it makes him feel noble; but using it on a daily basis seems impractical and risky.

As shown, the medical research novel offers a very suitable background against which the author, usually but not necessarily through the main character, can examine ideas about the workings of nature, fate, and God. In each case studied here, the medical researcher has, if not any acknowledged spiritual needs, at least some curiosity about a higher order. This group of novels presents several timeless topics of scientific as well as metaphysical interest: the origin of life, the existence of an ultimate authority which determines natural laws, the existence of a Master Plan and the individual's part in it, the possibility of more than one life on earth, the ultimate goal of human life, and the limits to the realm of scientific proof. Almost every novel addresses the possibility of reconciling scientific principles and supernatural beliefs.

Most of the novels do not, however, provide much discussion of the metaphysical questions which they raise. In general, the main characters' opinions are made known with little explanation or examination. To half of the chief characters mentioned here (and to other characters), agnosticism or atheism appears the only scientific position, and either nature or the human mind seems to be the highest authority. Yet the only one of these scientists who participates in serious theological discussions is Alex Addams, and he is already convinced that God is a human invention. To the central characters on the other side of the issue, there is no question about the existence of God but only a question about what, if anything, God does in present times. These medical scientists also offer little enlightenment in this matter. There is, of course, Fritz Wieser, who comes to a belief in the spiritual realm after the supernatural reveals itself to him; but his experience is hardly convincing to any reader who is not predisposed to a belief in reincarnation. The notion of fate as an independent power is accepted by none of the researchers; those who feel that life is predetermined also believe in God in some form. Georg Letham, with his unique viewpoint, links any apparent operations of fate or karma to nature or, tentatively, to an often malevolent deity. Of all the protagonists, only Letham examines spiritual matters with anything like scientific objectivity and persistence; and though he does a fair amount of soul-searching, the final state of his beliefs is not the result of any diligent quest.

In the cases of Letham and many others, parental instruction or the mentor's example exerts a greater influence on the formation of metaphysical beliefs than does medical science itself. In other words, the chief characters, being human, are subject to prejudices in these matters. Only Alex Addams is shown to have overcome the influence of his most significant other, and Addams is not free from bias in the supposed pure rationality of his agnosticism.

Of course, the authors' as well as the main characters' priorities keep medical research novels as a group from satisfactorily handling questions about the higher order. Most of the novelists obviously do not consider it appropriate—that is, realistic or otherwise artistically desirable—to depict a medical researcher devoting much time and energy to spiritual problems. In the main, the issues have been settled in advance and therefore take little of these scientists' attention away from the business at hand.

Conclusion

In order to characterize the special literary subset of medical research novels published in English or German from 1900 to 1950, this study has concentrated on the protagonists, examining the effects of medical research work on their 1) attitudes toward medicine and science; 2) self-images and attitudes toward life and success; 3) physical and mental health; 4) close relationships with other people; 5) attitudes toward social issues, culture, and recreation; and 6) beliefs about the ultimate authority. These effects vary from novel to novel because the central characters are conceived as distinctive individuals. On the other hand, there are definite similarities among the fictional medical scientists. Especially worthy of note in this regard is the fact that there are no significant differences in outlook between the main characters of the novels in English and those of the novels in German. Although the protagonists inevitably reveal distinguishing traces of national and ethnic character, they are united by bonds which cross boundaries of every kind.

In examining the consequences of the chief characters' commitment to medical science, this study has brought to light the many important issues which medical research novels present to their readers. Most of these topics are just as vital now as when the novels were written.

As might be expected, the subgenre provides an excellent forum for the discussion of basic philosophical issues in medicine and science. In every novel there is the overall theme of the actual versus the ideal qualities of a person who is both doctor and scientist, and in various ways the novels all show the importance of the individual physician-researcher vis-à-vis the research collective. Those central characters who are shown before they become involved with scientific work must determine the extent of their responsibilities to patients, and many feel morally obligated to provide help for more than just physical needs. A few of the physicians inwardly debate whether they are ever justified in not being completely open with a patient; and while honesty is generally considered the best policy, there are special cases which seem to warrant not telling the whole truth. In some of the novels, there is discussion of the merits of or the problems with specialization in medical science; broad experience is shown to be preferable for both doctor and researcher, and the trend toward very narrow specialization is generally considered harmful in medical practice but not in research. Of course, once the physician becomes interested in scientific investigation, he or she has other and probably harder decisions to make. Many of the main characters have a problem with dividing their time between research work and the treatment of patients; in most cases, the research becomes the chief concern. In a number of novels, medicine and science are shown to have other conflicts of interests as well. The heart of the matter is that the practitioner of medicine is supposed to be compassionate but the scientist dispassionate, and a person cannot be both at the same time. While medicine is concerned with the immediate goal of promoting the health of individual patients and saving lives at any cost, science is concerned with nothing but acquiring knowledge for the eventual good of humanity in general. Weighing the cost of scientific knowledge, some of the chief characters look at ethical issues such as vivisection, the use of human beings as experimental subjects, and science's responsibility for the laity's misuse of its discoveries. They can finally justify any means of generating and gathering potentially useful data except the use of unwitting or unwilling human subjects; and they would relieve science of the restriction of making only such discoveries as could never be used for evil purposes. Some of the researchers concern themselves with such elemental matters as defining the limits of science's domain and determining its ultimate effectiveness in controlling nature, but they do not allow any of the indications to disturb their work.

The medical scientist's introspection and reflections on life enrich literature in the same way as those of any other fictional character, and contemplative readers will find parallels between the lives of protagonists of medical research novels and their own lives. Like anyone else, medical researchers need high self-esteem in order to function optimally, and they base important decisions on their understanding of the meaning and purpose of life. As a group, they have the same range of altruistic and egoistic motivations as any other group of professionals which can claim to serve the best interests of humanity. As individuals, they define success in essentially the same ways as any other persons with a great drive to achieve. From many perspectives, then, the medical research novel can offer worthwhile insights into the challenges of living with oneself, with or without success.

Living with physical and mental occupational hazards is another timely topic which this literary subset is particularly well suited to treat. By extension, its central characters represent any type of dedicated professional whose vocation can have high physical and emotional costs. They also demonstrate the irony unique to their own occupation: because they are so thoroughly engrossed in making the world a healthier place in which to live, most of them either cannot or will not take proper care of their own health. Both painstakingly thorough in their research and keenly determined to finish their projects as soon as possible, they tend to overwork themselves. Many of them become chain smokers, caffeine addicts, insomniacs, and/or neurotics for at least a short period of time. A few abuse alcohol or other drugs or both. One of the protagonists has a complete nervous breakdown, and two of them are driven insane by frustration. Many risk their lives in the conduct of their research, and several use themselves as experimental subjects.

The health of the main character's relationships with other people is also an important concern of the medical research novel. The doctor-scientist is a good representative of any dedicated professional who is extremely jealous of his or her time but unable to live without human companionship. The subgenre illustrates well what can happen to the relationships of a person whose work becomes all-consuming. Specifically, it shows, in most cases, the dedicated researcher's inability to maintain many close friendships or a satisfying home life for very long. The high rate of separation and divorce among such professionals is evident in this group of novels. Notably and understandably, parents, siblings, or children of the protagonist are seldom developed as full characters. On the other hand, the value of a supportive and companionable co-worker is underscored in almost every novel. And in most cases where the chief character's trusted colleague or assistant is of the opposite sex, a romantic interest develops as well.

The medical scientist's relationships to matters of economics, politics, and culture are not emphasized in most of the novels, nor does the subject of recreation receive much attention. Because of every central character's absorption in medical research, the subgenre is not particularly well suited to explore such matters. Nevertheless, some of the main characters state opinions on quite a range of societal concerns, and some of the narrators offer their own insights rather directly. Three protagonists back up ideas with action on behalf of colleagues who are treated unfairly. All in all, six of the novels give quite a good idea of the social and political climate of the times. *The Fire and the Wood,* for example, gives the reader an authentic-feeling experience of life in Germany in 1933, when all rights of Jews were officially abolished. *Narkose* presents a good deal of information about Boston and the United States in general between the War of 1812 and the Civil War. Perhaps the most important and most obvious social question addressed in the subgenre is that of the scientist's role in society, the consensus being that the medical researcher's virtual isolation from general human affairs for long periods of time is as it must be. The medical scientist serves humanity best by doing his or her job.

Some indications of the spiritual climate of the times are given in this group of novels, but it does not realize its potential for presenting the issues of scientific materialism's dispute with spirituality of any kind. Only *Arrowsmith, Doctor Addams,* and *Georg Letham, Arzt und Mörder* treat more than superficially the scientist's difficulties in believing in a personal First Cause or an overall governing power of the universe, beyond nature or the human mind. *Georg Letham* is the only novel which shows a real struggle going on within the soul of the protagonist, and this struggle is given up soon enough. In matters of metaphysics, most of the main characters' minds are already made up, one way or another. Seven protagonists, at some point in the novels, are shown to believe in God; eight either call themselves agnostics or give the impression of being such; and the two remaining are not sure about the existence of God but make no effort to investigate. None of the medical researchers believes in fate as an actual independent force. Scientific skepticism with regard to the spiritual plane is well illustrated; but because of the novelists' and the chief characters' priorities and prejudices (and because of science's inadequacy for dealing with metaphysical problems), scientific curiosity and objectivity are not.

The medical research novel has not yet exhausted all of its possibilities. The findings of medical science, which now make the news more often than ever, and the speculation and controversy which greet them are good material for novels. The medical researcher, continually changing with the world, should have an enduring place as a central character in fiction. Though the medical research novel has changed since 1950, it certainly has not died out. Four notable examples which have achieved great popularity and made a dramatic impact are Michael Crichton's *The Andromeda Strain* (1969), Robin Cook's *Coma* (1977), Paddy Chayefsky's *Altered States* (1978), and Robin Cook's *Outbreak* (1987). These offerings indicate that the subgenre is increasingly challenging the distinction between medical science and science fiction and that it has begun to expand the definition of medical research to include medical detective work. The authors of future additions to this subset of literature should find a wealth of possibilities in such contemporary topics as incurable disease, environmental pollution, genetic engineering, the prolonging of life, life on other planets, and medical technology used for individuals' criminal purposes or nations' military goals.

Appendix

For the reasons given below, the following books were not included in this study although they shed light on important aspects of researchers and medical science. The books are grouped according to their disqualifications.

Group A: In each of these novels, medical research plays a minor role in either the plot of the novel or in the life of the protagonist, or both.

Adams, Samuel Hopkins. *Canal Town.* New York: Random House, 1944.
Arey, John Stuart. *There Was No Yesterday.* Garden City, New York: Doubleday, Doran and Co., 1944.
Avera, Homer. *Dr. Roger's Ordeal.* New York: John H. Hopkins, 1938.
Basso, Hamilton. *Days Before Lent.* New York: Charles Scribner's Sons, 1939.
Blake, George. *Young Malcolm.* New York and London: Harper and Brothers, 1927.
Cronin, A.J. *The Citadel.* Boston: Little, Brown and Co., 1937.
_____ *Grand Canary.* Boston: Little, Brown and Co., 1933.
Douglas, Lloyd C. *Disputed Passage.* New York: Grosset & Dunlap, 1939.
Lieferant, Henry, and Sylvia Lieferant. *One Enduring Purpose.* New York: Dutton, 1941.
Lorenz, Friedrich. *Zwillinge aus einem Ei. Der Roman eines biologischen Experiments.* Wien und Berlin: Paul Neff Verlag, 1950.
Roberts, W. Adolphe. *Creole Dusk: A New Orleans Novel of the '80s.* Indianapolis and New York: The Bobbs-Merrill Co., 1948.
Weiss, Ernst. *Der arme Verschwender.* Amsterdam, 1936; rpt. Frankfurt: Suhrkamp, 1982.

Group B: In each of these novels, the research work is of benefit to medical science, but the protagonist is neither a physician nor a medical student.

Brandt, Herbert. *Blutgruppe AB.* Berlin und Leipzig: Vier Tannen Verlag, 1943.
Dahmen, Walter. *Mitte des Lebens.* Breslau: Korn, 1941.
Dominik, Hans. *Lebensstrahlen.* Berlin: Scherl, 1938.
Fairway, Sidney. *The Long Tunnel.* Garden City, New York: Doubleday, Doran and Co., 1936.
Walde, Hilde. *Die andere Maria.* Breslau: Korn, 1940.
Weiss, Ernst. *Die Galeere.* 1913; rpt. Frankfurt: Suhrkamp, 1982.

Group C: Though recommended reading, these two works are not novels. The first is a straightforward autobiography of literary quality. The second has elements of good fiction writing but is a thinly disguised autobiography.

Much, Hans. *Arzt und Mensch. Das Lebensbuch eines Forschers und Helfers.* Dresden: Reissner, 1932.
Zinsser, Hans. *As I Remember Him: The Biography of R. S.* Boston: Little, Brown and Co., 1940.

The following are *possible* medical research novels, as indicated in each case by at least one listing in an annotated bibliography. Unfortunately, copies of the books themselves were not obtained.

Balchin, Nigel. *Who Is My Neighbor?* Boston: Houghton Mifflin, 1950.
Fairway, Sidney. *Dr. Budleigh's Heritage.* London: Kinsey, 1934.
Hartmann, Hans. *Vitamine. Auf der Spur des Lebensgeheimnisses.* Stuttgart: Union, 1939.
Horler, Sydney. *The Charlatan.* Boston: Little, Brown and Co., 1934.
Katz, Georg. *Lotte Landes Traum vom Glück.* Berlin: Schwetschke, 1915.
Löbel, Josef. *Lebensretter. Detektivromane aus der Geschichte der Medizin.* Zürich: Bibliothek Zeitgenossischer Werke, 1935.
Nassauer, Max. *Das Nessushemd.* Dresden: Reissner, 1913.
Reichenwallner, Balduin. *Ein Experiment des Doktors Sargillac.* Wiesbaden: Voigt, 1919.
Stiebing, Martin. *Wanderung zum Ich.* Berlin: Keil, 1942.
Uller, Tyll. *Semmelweis. Der Roman seines heroischen Wirkens.* Berlin: Hanseatischer Rechts- und Wirtschafts-Verlag, 1943.
Unger, Hellmuth. *Louis Pasteur. Bildnis eines Genies.* Hamburg: Hoffman und Campe, 1950.

Notes

Introduction
[1]Enid Rhodes Peschel, ed., *Medicine and Literature* (New York: Neale Watson, 1980).

Joanne Trautmann and Carol Pollard, *Literature and Medicine: An Annotated Bibliography*, rev. ed. (Pittsburgh: U of Pittsburgh P, 1982).

Jeffrey Meyers, *Disease and the Novel, 1880-1960* (London: Macmillan, 1985).

Bruce Clarke and Wendell Aycock, eds., *The Body and the Text: Comparative Essays in Literature and Medicine* (Lubbock: Texas Tech UP, 1990).

[2]Of the 379 novels about doctors which Evelyn Rivers Wilbanks lists in her article "The Physician in the American Novel, 1870-1955" in *Bulletin of Bibliography* 22.7 (1958), seventeen were published from 1877 to 1899, and 361 were published from 1900 to 1955 (one was not dated). Although Wilbanks says in her introduction, "The first prerequisite in the selection of the books was that the physician be the main character," it is uncertain how many of her entries would qualify as doctor novels as defined here. She includes, for example, Carson McCullers' *The Heart is a Lonely Hunter*, and her bibliography also includes at least one other novel in which the physician is not the protagonist. Wilbanks states openly that she has "accepted the authority and decisions of the secondary sources which listed novels about physicians." Her use of the term "American novel" must also be questioned because her list includes the English translations of at least two foreign novels, Hans Carossa's *Doctor Gion* (from the German *Der Arzt Gion*) and Willy Corsari's *Man without Uniform* (from the Dutch *De Man zonder Uniform*). Still, even after allowing for error, one can see the overall indication of the numbers from this ambitious bibliographic undertaking.

There is a comparable listing for the physician in German literature, with citations from 1802 to 1952. Franz Anselm Schmitt's *Beruf und Arbeit in deutscher Erzählung: Ein literarisches Lexikon* (Stuttgart: Hiersemann Verlag, 1952), which lists books and stories about people in particular jobs and professions, has one section headed "Arzt" and others with headings for various medical specialists. Unless one has read all of the novels cited, it is impossible to say how many of them fit this study's definition of the doctor novel. However, the numbers from Schmitt's bibliography are comparable to those from Wilbanks': twelve such novels published before 1900 versus more than 200 novels published since then.

[3]To be sure, there are novels whose only medical researcher-protagonists have never been physicians or even medical students but are instead biologists, chemists, or physicists. For the purposes of this study, such novels are considered members of another subset of the larger group of scientific research novels and are not dealt with here. There are also novels which have one or more protagonists in addition to the one who is a medical researcher. Such novels are included in this study as medical research novels: Vicki Baum's *Zwischenfall in Lohwinckel*, Hans Rabl's *Die Trennung*, Rudolf Daumann's *Patrouille gegen den Tod*, R.C. Hutchinson's *The*

Fire and the Wood, and Mildred Walker's *Medical Meeting.* In discussion of these novels, the researcher is the only protagonist mentioned unless there is a specific reason for mentioning another.

⁴Using the bibliographic tools cited in Note 2 above, as well as Trautmann and Pollard's annotated bibliography (see Note 1) and Richard Robert Malmsheimer's dissertation, "From Rappaccini to Marcus Welby: The Evolution of an Image" (Univ. of Minnesota 1978), one can get at least an approximate count of medical research novels published before 1900. However, as stated in Note 2, the only way of getting truly accurate numbers is to read each novel in question. Failing that, one must rely on plot summaries or other specific remarks in secondary sources. Trautmann and Pollard give synopses of all the literary works they list, and Malmsheimer gives at least some analysis of most of the novels listed in his dissertation's bibliography. Some of Schmitt's citations are annotated very briefly, but Wilbanks' have no annotation at all.

Certainly, not all of the twelve pre-1900 novels listed under Schmitt's general heading "Arzt" are medical research novels. Schmitt lists only one of these novels under the heading "Forscher" (which also includes explorers and other types of researchers). However, since some verified medical research novels published after 1900 appear under only one of the above headings, Schmitt's cross-referencing proves unreliable.

One can say with near certainty that there were fewer than ten American medical research novels published before 1900. Of the seventeen pre-1900 novels which Wilbanks lists, at least eight can be eliminated by the use of information in Malmsheimer, Trautmann and Pollard, and book reviews.

Determining the number of British medical research novels, whenever published, is even more difficult. It appears that no single comprehensive list of British novels about doctors exists, although a fairly complete list of such novels published after 1907 can be compiled from *Book Review Digest.*

Two important nineteenth-century prototypes of the medical research novel come readily to mind: Mary Wollstonecraft Shelley's *Frankenstein* (1816) and Robert Louis Stevenson's *Dr. Jekyll and Mr. Hyde* (1886). One would have to stretch the definition to include them in the subgenre: the protagonist of the former is not exactly a physician, and the latter is really a novelette rather than a short novel.

⁵Although this study concentrates on the effects of medical research on people in the profession, it recognizes the fact that the type of person who becomes a doctor-researcher already has certain characteristics which may or may not change. Care is taken not to attribute attitudes or other facts of researchers' lives to the demands and rewards of the profession except as warranted by the novels.

Chapter One

¹Naturally, this career fulfills certain ego needs as well. Some of these less noble-sounding motivations are presented later in this chapter. In Chapter Two, there is additional discussion of researchers' drives.

²Sinclair Lewis, *Arrowsmith* (1925; rpt. New York: Harcourt, Brace, 1964). Page references appear in the text.

³Irving Fineman, *Doctor Addams* (New York: Random House, 1939) 58. Subsequent page references appear in the text.

⁴Alan Hart, *The Undaunted* (New York: W.W. Norton, 1936) 229. Subsequent page references appear in the text.

[5]Adolf Koelsch, *Narkose. Der Roman vom Kampf gegen den Schmerz* (Zürich: Albert Müller Verlag, 1938). The protagonist of this novel is William Thomas Green Morton (1819-1868), who in 1846 introduced the use of ether as a general anesthetic.

Theo Malade, *Semmelweis, der Retter der Mütter. Der Roman eines ärztlichen Lebens*, 2. Aufl. (München: J.F. Lehmanns Verlag, 1924). This novel and the one listed immediately below portray Ignaz Philipp Semmelweis (1818-1865), who in 1847 discovered the cause of puerperal fever and introduced basic hospital sanitation.

Morton Thompson, *The Cry and the Covenant* (Garden City, NY: Doubleday, 1949). Page references appear in the text.

Hellmuth Unger, *Helfer der Menschheit. Der Lebensroman Robert Kochs* (Leipzig: Verlag der Buchhandlung des Verbandes der Ärzte Deutschlands, 1929). Page references appear in the text. Robert Koch (1843-1910) has many discoveries to his credit but is probably best known for identifying the tubercle bacillus and developing the first tuberculin. He was awarded the Nobel Prize for physiology and medicine in 1905.

[6]Betina Ewerbeck, *Angela Koldewey. Roman einer jungen Ärztin* (1939; rpt. Ulm: Aegis Verlag, 1950).

W.B. Erlin, *Die Spur* (Berlin: Die Neue Lese, 1947). Page references appear in the text. W.B. Erlin is the pseudonym of Walter B. Schirmeier (1902-   ).

Rudolf Heinrich Daumann, *Patrouille gegen den Tod. Ein utopischer Roman*, 21.-60. Tausend. (Berlin: Schützen Verlag, 1939). Page references appear in the text.

[7]R.C. Hutchinson, *The Fire and the Wood: A Love Story* (London, 1940; rpt. New York, Literary Guild of America, 1940). Page references appear in the text.

Ernst Weiss, *Georg Letham, Arzt und Mörder* (Wien: 1931; rpt. Frankfurt, Suhrkamp, 1982). Page references appear in the text.

Hermann Hoster, *Viele sind berufen. Ein Roman unter Ärzten*, 27.-38. Auflage (Leipzig: Paul List Verlag, 1933). Page references appear in the text. Hermann Hoster is the pseudonym of Hermann Koch (1896-1943). Gregor Martin Bertram is the assumed name of the chief character, Martin Klaus.

[8]The following are at some time general practitioners: Martin Arrowsmith, Richard Cameron, Robert Koch, Nikolas Persenthein, Walter Töpfer, and Fritz Wieser. These others have rather broad medical backgrounds: Alex Addams, Martin Bertram, Angela Koldewey, Georg Letham, and Robert Shannon.

[9]Hans Rabl, *Die Trennung* (Berlin: Paul Neff Verlag, 1936). Page references appear in the text.

[10]Mildred Walker, *Medical Meeting* (New York: Harcourt, Brace, 1949) 108. Subsequent page references appear in the text.

[11]Georg Letham, the only main character whose final attitudes and actions might bring this statement into question, has a great deal of sympathy for at least some of the yellow fever victims he attends.

[12]This is true for Henry Baker, Richard Cameron, Nikolas Persenthein, and Josef Zeppichmann. In addition, Cameron and Zeppichmann each make a good friend of a human experimental subject. Persenthein, however, is interested in his subject more as the living proof of his theory than as a person.

Persenthein is the protagonist of Vicki Baum's *Zwischenfall in Lohwinckel* (Berlin: Verlag Ullstein, 1930). Page references appear in the text.

[13]The chief characters of *The Undaunted, The Fire and the Wood*, and *Georg Letham, Arzt und Mörder* use one or more unwitting human subjects. However, they all come to recognize their moral culpability in this practice.

The situation in *Viele sind berufen,* however, is ambiguous. Bertram thoroughly tests his anesthetic on animals and tests it once on himself before demonstrating it in operations on other humans, but there is no indication of the surgery patients' prior knowledge of and consent to the use of Bertram's experimental Narkophen on them. Two other medical researchers argue the morality of testing new procedures on humans, but Bertram does not take a definite stand on the issue.

[14]Ludwig Anton, *Die japanische Pest* (Leipzig: Ernst Keils Nachfolger [August Scherl], 1925).

[15]In Chapter Three of this study, there will be further discussion of the main characters who knowingly sacrifice their health and risk their lives for the sake of their research.

Chapter Two

[1]Betina Ewerbeck, *Angela Koldewey. Roman einer jungen Ärztin* (1939; rpt. Ulm: Aegis Verlag, 1950). Page references appear in the text.

[2]As mentioned in Note 3 of this study's introduction, some of the novels have two or more chief characters. Some of these other protagonists are women but not doctors involved in research. (The two who come closest to this criterion are laboratory assistants.) On the other hand, some of the novels feature female medical researchers who are not main characters.

[3]In the German system, after a medical student passes the *Staatsexamen,* he or she is licensed as an *Arzt* or *Ärztin* to practice medicine. An Arzt/Ärztin may then elect to pursue a doctorate, which requires specialized research work and a dissertation. Strictly speaking, only a person with the Dr. med. degree is a *Doktor.*

[4]*Taber's Cyclopedic Medical Dictionary,* Edition 15, (Philadelphia: F.A. Davis, 1985) 706, defines malignant granuloma as lymphogranulomatosis or Hodgkin's disease.

[5]Angela contracts malignant granuloma on a trip to see a victim of that disease. Strictly speaking, it is not the research work itself but a sudden chill which causes her non-contagious illness.

[6]Sinclair Lewis, *Arrowsmith* (1925; rpt. New York: Harcourt, Brace, 1964). Page references appear in the text.

[7]A.J. Cronin, *Shannon's Way* (Boston: Little, Brown, 1948). Page references appear in the text.

[8]Robert Shannon's overall similarity to Martin Arrowsmith was noted by several contemporary reviewers of *Shannon's Way.*

[9]Ernst Weiss, *Georg Letham, Arzt und Mörder* (Wien: 1931; rpt. Frankfurt: Suhrkamp, 1982). Page references appear in the text.

[10]R.C. Hutchinson, *The Fire and the Wood: A Love Story* (London, 1940; rpt. New York, Literary Guild of America, 1940).

[11]Morton Thompson, *The Cry and the Covenant* (Garden City, New York: Doubleday, 1949). Page references appear in the text.

Theo Malade, *Semmelweis, der Retter der Mütter. Der Roman eines ärztlichen Lebens,* 2. Aufl. (München: J.F. Lehmanns Verlag, 1924). Page references appear in the text.

[12]Hans Rabl, *Die Trennung* (Berlin: Paul Neff Verlag, 1936). Page references appear in the text.

[13]Irving Fineman, *Doctor Addams* (New York: Random House, 1939). Page references appear in the text.

[14]W.B. Erlin, *Die Spur* (Berlin: Die Neue Lese, 1947). Page references appear in the text.

[15]Mildred Walker, *Medical Meeting* (New York: Harcourt, Brace, 1949). Page references appear in the text.

In each of the following novels as well, the protagonist just misses being credited with a discovery when another scientist reports the same (or better) results first: *Arrowsmith*, *Shannon's Way*, *Georg Letham*, *Arzt und Mörder*, and Vicki Baum's *Zwischenfall in Lohwinckel* (Berlin: Verlag Ullstein, 1930).

In four other novels, the main characters have trouble gaining the medical establishment's recognition of either the validity of their research results or their own role in the discovery in question. In both *The Cry and the Covenant* and *Retter der Mütter*, Semmelweis can convince very few of his European colleagues of the urgency of adopting his antiseptic procedure; therefore, thousands of patients die needlessly each year. In Hellmuth Unger's *Helfer der Menschheit. Der Lebensroman Robert Kochs* (Leipzig: Verlag der Buchhandlung des Verbandes der Ärzte Deutschlands, 1929), the hero's first findings are not accepted by the scientific establishment for a long time, despite his now-undisputed proofs. After Morton in Adolf Koelsch's *Narkose. Der Roman vom Kampf gegen den Schmerz* (Zürich: Albert Müller Verlag, 1938) makes his discovery, he spends virtually the rest of his life defending his claim to priority.

[16]Baker refers to the French physician Pierre Charles Alexandre Louis (1787-1872), who made important observations concerning tuberculosis and who is considered the founder of medical statistics.

[17]Hellmuth Unger, *Helfer der Menschheit* 124. Subsequent page references appear in the text.

[18]Alex Addams and Robert Koch also reach very enviable positions in their careers. The following chief characters are offered some if not all of the rewards mentioned, but they experience this type of success to a somewhat lesser degree than Arrowsmith: William T.G. Morton; Hans Lennhoff; Walter Töpfer; Martin Bertram in Hermann Hoster's *Viele sind berufen. Ein Roman unter Ärzten* 27.-38. Auflage (Leipzig: Paul List Verlag, 1933); Richard Cameron in Alan Hart's *The Undaunted* (New York: W. W. Norton, 1936); and Alfried Kalsten in Rudolf Heinrich Daumann's *Patrouille gegen den Tod. Ein utopischer Roman* 21.-60. Tausend (Berlin: Schützen Verlag, 1939).

[19]Persenthein is the main character of *Zwischenfall in Lohwinckel*.

[20]Rudolf Heinrich Daumann, *Patrouille gegen den Tod* 312.

[21]Ludwig Anton, *Die japanische Pest* (Leipzig: Ernst Keils Nachfolger [August Scherl], 1925). Wieser is also offered a very good position with a sanitarium in Berlin, but he dislikes the feeling of being forever beholden to the doctor recommending him for the job and to the doctors who would refer patients to him.

Chapter Three

[1]The nine are Martin Arrowsmith, Martin Bertram, Alfried Kalsten, Robert Koch, Georg Letham, William T.G. Morton, Ignaz Philipp Semmelweis, Fritz Wieser, and Josef Zeppichmann.

[2]Hellmuth Unger, *Helfer der Menschheit. Der Lebensroman Robert Kochs* (Leipzig: Verlag der Buchhandlung des Verbandes der Ärzte Deutschlands, 1929) 107. Subsequent page references appear in the text.

[3]Theo Malade, *Semmelweis, der Retter der Mütter. Der Roman eines ärztlichen Lebens* 2. Aufl. (München: J.F. Lehmanns Verlag, 1924) 101.

[4]Hermann Hoster, *Viele sind berufen. Ein Roman unter Ärzten* 27.-38. Auflage (Leipzig: Paul List Verlag, 1933) 63. Subsequent page references appear in the text.

[5]Sinclair Lewis, *Arrowsmith* (1925; rpt. New York: Harcourt, Brace, 1964) 429. Subsequent page references appear in the text.

[6]W.B. Erlin, *Die Spur* (Berlin: Die Neue Lese, 1947) 22. Subsequent page references appear in the text.

[7]Vicki Baum, *Zwischenfall in Lohwinckel* (Berlin: Verlag Ullstein, 1930) 37. Subsequent page references appear in the text.

[8]Ernst Weiss, *Georg Letham, Arzt und Mörder* (Wien: 1931; rpt. Frankfurt, Suhrkamp, 1982). The subsequent page reference appears in the text.

[9]R.C. Hutchinson, *The Fire and the Wood: A Love Story* (London, 1940; rpt. New York, Literary Guild of America, 1940).

[10]The debilitating effects of tropical heat and humidity are noted in some detail in *Georg Letham, Arzt und Mörder*, but they of themselves represent no major health concern for Letham.

[11]Morton Thompson, *The Cry and the Covenant* (Garden City, New York: Doubleday, 1949). In *Retter der Mütter* Semmelweis' death is treated as accidental.

[12]Adolf Koelsch, *Narkose. Der Roman vom Kampf gegen den Schmerz* (Zürich: Albert Müller Verlag, 1938).

[13]Rudolf Heinrich Daumann, *Patrouille gegen den Tod. Ein utopischer Roman* 21.-60. Tausend (Berlin: Schützen Verlag, 1939).

[14]Ludwig Anton, *Die japanische Pest* (Leipzig: Ernst Keils Nachfolger [August Scherl], 1925).

[15]Mildred Walker, *Medical Meeting* (New York: Harcourt, Brace, 1949).

[16]A.J. Cronin, *Shannon's Way* (Boston: Little, Brown, 1948).

[17]Martin Bertram's dizziness is associated with a cold or flu, for which stress, malnutrition, and low resistance due to overwork are responsible.

[18]Two notable exceptions are Alex Addams in Irving Fineman's *Doctor Addams* (New York: Random House, 1949) and Fritz Wieser. Addams, 45 years old, is trim, energetic, and virile. Although his working hours are sometimes irregular, his routine is obviously a healthful one. His life is very sane and orderly, and he even makes time for handball and swimming with some regularity. Wieser, at least while conducting research for the Japanese government, has a well-balanced daily schedule of work, meals, exercise, and rest.

[19]Alan Hart, *The Undaunted* (New York: W.W. Norton, 1936). Page references appear in the text.

[20]An entertaining depiction of what could be called desperate caffeine abuse is provided by the narrator of *Die Spur*, who tells of the dangerously strong coffee which the protagonist's laboratory assistant brews to revive Lennhoff and himself. The powerful concentrate, "der alles Sonstige an Bitterkeit, Giftgehalt und Stärke weit in den Schatten stellte," is referred to as "Teufelstrank" and "Rosskur" (91).

[21]Ignorant of the ways of business, Morton has patented a superfluous apparatus for administering ether but has publicly disclosed the name of his anesthetic and shown how it works.

Chapter Four

[1]Some main characters have an occupationally related emotional disturbance which makes it unpleasant for others to be around them. In most of these cases, the condition is temporary. The focus in this chapter, however, is on the more common and more basic interpersonal problems caused by researchers' involvement in their

work. To avoid repetition of material in Chapter Three of this study, the present chapter omits specific mention of the changes which protagonists' personality disorders make in their relationships with other people.

[2]Despite the fact that lovers and marriage partners can and should be friends, the word *friend* in this chapter will not be applied to any person with whom a protagonist has an erotic relationship.

[3]W.B. Erlin, *Die Spur* (Berlin: Die Neue Lese, 1947). Page references appear in the text.

[4]Hellmuth Unger, *Helfer der Menschheit. Der Lebensroman Robert Kochs* (Leipzig: Verlag der Buchhandlung des Verbandes der Ärzte Deutschlands, 1929). Page references appear in the text.

[5]All of the seventeen main characters except Bertram, Kalsten, and Shannon marry, and these three are about to be married at the end of their respective novels. Martin Arrowsmith and Robert Koch marry twice. Those who become divorced are Hans Lennhoff, Robert Koch, Martin Arrowsmith (from his second wife), and William T.G. Morton.

In Ernst Weiss's *Georg Letham, Arzt und Mörder* (Wien: 1931; rpt. Frankfurt, Suhrkamp, 1982), the main character murders his wife because he wants to be free of her smothering love and he needs the money from her life insurance to finance his experiments.

[6]The two medical scientists in question are Nikolas Persenthein and Walter Töpfer, of Vicki Baum's *Zwischenfall in Lohwinckel* (Berlin: Verlag Ullstein, 1930) and Hans Rabl's *Die Trennung* (Berlin: Paul Neff Verlag, 1936) respectively.

[7]Irving Fineman, *Doctor Addams* (New York: Random House, 1939). Subsequent page references appear in the text. Alex Addams and his wife Louise separate, not because of his preoccupation with research but because neither can fulfill the other's personal needs. It may be argued, however, that Addams' scientific mindset and consequent priorities are responsible for his not finding a solution to his marital problem.

[8]As mentioned earlier, Leora Arrowsmith dies of the plague during the epidemic which provides human subjects for Martin's important experiment. Years after remarrying, Robert Koch dies of a heart condition brought on in part by his missions in the tropics. Ignaz Philipp Semmelweis dies of septicemia resulting from a cut received in his battle against puerperal fever. Josef Zeppichmann dies of tuberculosis, which he has evidently contracted while doctoring his experimental subject and future wife, Minna. Minna dies of the disease at about the time he does. As seen earlier, Angela Koldewey dies of malignant granuloma, for which she has hoped to discover a cure; but her illness is not really caused by her research work.

[9]Richard Cameron and Fritz Wieser, in Alan Hart's *The Undaunted* (New York: W.W. Norton, 1936) and Ludwig Anton's *Die japanische Pest* (Leipzig: Ernst Keils Nachfolger [August Scherl], 1925) respectively, have each been married a relatively short time, even at the end of the novel.

[10]In the case of Walter Töpfer, however, there is an ironic twist. Because his wife Eva understands how important his work is, she is willing to give him up rather than hinder his research. Indeed, he must talk her out of giving him a type of freedom that he does not want.

[11]Sinclair Lewis, *Arrowsmith* (1925; rpt. New York: Harcourt, Brace, 1964). Page references appear in the text.

[12]Hermann Hoster, *Viele sind berufen. Ein Roman unter Ärzten* 27.-38. Auflage (Leipzig: Paul List Verlag, 1933).

[13]A.J. Cronin, *Shannon's Way* (Boston: Little, Brown, 1948).

[14]Morton Thompson, *The Cry and the Covenant* (Garden City, NY: Doubleday, 1949).

Theo Malade, *Semmelweis, der Retter der Mütter. Der Roman eines ärztlichen Lebens* 2. Aufl. (München: J.F. Lehmanns Verlag, 1924).

[15]Mildred Walker, *Medical Meeting* (New York: Harcourt, Brace, 1949). Page references appear in the text.

[16]Betina Ewerbeck, *Angela Koldewey. Roman einer jungen Ärztin* (1939; rpt. Ulm: Aegis Verlag, 1950).

[17]The eight who have children are Martin Arrowsmith, Henry Baker, Robert Koch, Angela Koldewey, William T.G. Morton, Nikolas Persenthein, Ignaz Philipp Semmelweis, and Walter Töpfer. Fritz Wieser's wife is pregnant but does not have her baby by the end of the novel.

[18]Leora Arrowsmith and Louise Addams become physically incapable of bearing children. Richard and Judith Cameron's baby, like the Arrowsmiths', is stillborn.

[19]Angela Koldewey's child also has another and much greater importance to her, as discussed in Chapter Two of this study.

[20]The main characters of *Doctor Addams*, *The Cry and the Covenant*, and *Angela Koldewey* maintain very warm relationships with their parents, though mostly by mail, for as long as the parents live. Addams, however, has grown away from his father's influence, in part because he has become increasingly interested in the theoretical part of medical science while the elder Addams has remained a medical practitioner.

In Rudolf Daumann's *Patrouille gegen den Tod* (Berlin: Schützen Verlag, 1939), one of the chief characters, Robert Dobbertin, feels that he should spend much more time with his convalescing father but also finds himself at the most critical point in his vitally important research project. However, as a biologist and not a physician, Dobbertin is not a protagonist who directly concerns this study.

In *Shannon's Way* the hero's parents have died, but his grandmother is like a mother to him. She takes a very active interest in his affairs, and he maintains an appreciative, dutiful, and respectful attitude toward her.

In R.C. Hutchinson's *The Fire and the Wood: A Love Story* (London, 1940; rpt. New York, Literary Guild of America, 1940), Josef Zeppichmann is once shown reading a letter from his parents and contemplating a dutifully affectionate answer. However, determined to ''be somebody'' someday by means of an important medical discovery, he deplores everything and everyone back home. He tries to remove from his speech, manners, and dress all traces of his humble upbringing.

Georg Letham, exiled to another continent and totally absorbed in the yellow fever problem, feels that he has lost all connection to the past and to his homeland. He claims, in fact, to have forgotten what his father looks like (495). The early part of the narrative, however, emphasizes the father's role in the formation of the son's character and thereby provides the subgenre's best study of parental influence.

[21]In only three novels is the chief character, as an adult, shown making any contact with one or more siblings: *The Cry and the Covenant*, *Doctor Addams*, and *Georg Letham, Arzt und Mörder*. Although Semmelweis tries to locate all of his brothers and sisters when he returns to Hungary, he sees only one married sister on rare occasions. In Alex Addams' case, the contact is forced; that is, he sees his brother and his sister only because he has come home for their father's funeral. The narrator of *Doctor Addams*, unique in this regard, explicitly comments on the fact that the siblings of the protagonist have no real conception of the work he does.

Georg Letham's brother is briefly significant in the plot of that novel, but the main character, exiled for life, effectively terminates their relationship by not writing.

Walter Töpfer in *Die Trennung* converses twice with a male cousin, once before and once after his research project. The cousin is important to the plot because he takes over Töpfer's practice while Töpfer is away and because his wife helps save the Töpfers' marriage.

[22]Adolf Koelsch, *Narkose. Der Roman vom Kampf gegen den Schmerz* (Zürich: Albert Müller Verlag, 1938).

[23]The six who do maintain one or more such relationships are Martin Arrowsmith, Martin Bertram, Richard Cameron, Georg Letham, Ignaz Philipp Semmelweis, and Robert Shannon.

[24]Those who are considered "best friends" here are quite intimate companions and confidants. Only Arrowsmith, Bertram, Letham, Semmelweis, and Shannon have best friends.

The term *colleagues* here is used to mean co-workers in the cause of medical research. Georg Letham makes the acquaintance of his best friend at a time when neither of them is active in research. However, they work in the same laboratory on the same project during the main part of the novel. Semmelweis' best friend Markussovsky is a doctor but not a researcher. Nevertheless, he gives Semmelweis moral and financial support as well as introductions to other benefactors, and he writes articles which help spread the doctrine of antisepsis.

[25]In other novels besides *Doctor Addams, Arrowsmith,* and *Georg Letham,* this type of relationship is suggested but not developed by the narrator.

[26]Of these three main characters, only Arrowsmith has lost his real father before getting to know the older researcher. However, Addams and Letham have both broken away from the influence of their fathers.

[27]Three other protagonists make such acquaintances but not because of the research work itself. While still a resident and not yet a researcher, Nikolas Persenthein meets Elisabeth, who later becomes his wife. Similarly, William T.G. Morton meets his future wife when he is a doctor's assistant and has not yet begun his research. Although Hans Lennhoff has been conducting his experimentation for some time before he meets Renate, they become acquainted at a party and not at his place of work. It should also be mentioned here that Martin Arrowsmith, whose relationship with Joyce is indicated in the text, is a medical student when he meets Leora, then a probationer nurse.

[28]This pattern is also seen in *Narkose.* Morton's cause is greatly helped by his young wife Madeleine's financial contribution.

Chapter Five

[1]The term *economics* here refers to the national or international economic situation and not to anyone's personal finances. *Culture* in this context refers to ethnic heritage as well as refinement of manners, tastes, and the mind.

[2]R.C. Hutchinson, *The Fire and the Wood: A Love Story* (London, 1940; rpt. New York, Literary Guild of America, 1940). Page references appear in the text.

Josef Zeppichmann's desire for fame, social standing, etc., discussed in Chapter Two of this study, is in no way denied here; but Josef is willing to forego all of life's rewards until after the completion of his project.

[3]Mildred Walker, *Medical Meeting* (New York: Harcourt, Brace and Co., 1949). Page references appear in the text.

[4]Betina Ewerbeck, *Angela Koldewey. Roman einer jungen Ärztin* (1939; rpt. Ulm: Aegis Verlag, 1950). The page reference appears in the text.

[5]W.B. Erlin, *Die Spur* (Berlin: Die Neue Lese, 1947). Page references appear in the text.

[6]Vicki Baum, *Zwischenfall in Lohwinckel* (Berlin: Verlag Ullstein, 1930). Page references appear in the text.

[7]Ernst Weiss, *Georg Letham, Arzt und Mörder* (Wien: 1931; rpt. Frankfurt, Suhrkamp, 1982). Page references appear in the text.

[8]Alan Hart, *The Undaunted* (New York: W.W. Norton, 1936). Page references appear in the text.

[9]Irving Fineman, *Doctor Addams* (New York: Random House, 1939). Page references appear in the text.

[10]Adolf Koelsch, *Narkose. Der Roman vom Kampf gegen den Schmerz* (Zürich: Albert Müller Verlag, 1938). Page references appear in the text.

Morton does not, however, continue to share Addams' faith in American society's—and the rest of humanity's—perfectability. His optimism is devastated by his bad experience in trying to reap the benefits of his research. When other men have claimed credit for and enjoyed profits from his discovery, and when much of the public has declared its moral opposition to the use of his anesthetic, Morton begins to see the human race as ungrateful, unworthy, and hopeless.

[11]Ludwig Anton, *Die japanische Pest* (Leipzig: Ernst Keils Nachfolger [August Scherl], 1925). Page references appear in the text.

[12]Hellmuth Unger, *Helfer der Menschheit. Der Lebensroman Robert Kochs* (Leipzig: Verlag der Buchhandlung des Verbandes der Ärzte Deutschlands, 1929). Page references appear in the text.

[13]Hermann Hoster, *Viele sind berufen. Ein Roman unter Ärzten*, 27.-38. Auflage (Leipzig: Paul List Verlag, 1933). Page references appear in the text.

[14]In this incident, not included in a later version of the novel, there are very chauvinistic overtones to the patriotism. Martin's views, however, are not as extreme as those of Wendemuth, who says, "Bielschowsky mag das Land, aus dem er herstammt, mit seinem Experiment vor der Welt kompromittieren, aber nicht unseres" (364). There is surely an implication in the fact that Bielschowsky, the least sympathetic character in the novel, is of Slavic (probably Russian) origin.

[15]Sinclair Lewis, *Arrowsmith* (1925; rpt. New York: Harcourt, Brace, 1964). Page references appear in the text.

[16]Morton Thompson, *The Cry and the Covenant* (Garden City, NY: Doubleday, 1949). All page references in this section of the text are from this novel.

Theo Malade, *Semmelweis, der Retter der Mütter. Der Roman eines ärztlichen Lebens*, 2. Aufl. (München: J.F. Lehmanns Verlag, 1924).

Chapter Six

[1]A perfect example of this type of usage is found in Alan Hart's *The Undaunted* (New York: W. W. Norton, 1936) 283. (Subsequent page references appear in the text.) In a moment of despondency, Richard Cameron thinks of "the familiar instruments of his craft" as "only the crude weapons with which blundering human beings tried to turn Fate aside." He does not, however, actually believe in predestination, nor does he mention fate in this way at any other time in the novel.

[2]Ernst Weiss, *George Letham, Arzt und Mörder* (Wien: 1931; rpt. Frankfurt, Suhrkamp, 1982). Page references appear in the text.

[3]Irving Fineman, *Doctor Addams* (New York: Random House, 1939). Page references appear in the text.

[4]Sinclair Lewis, *Arrowsmith* (1925; rpt. New York: Harcourt, Brace, 1964). Page references appear in the text.

[5]Ludwig Anton, *Die japanische Pest* (Leipzig: Ernst Keils Nachfolger [August Scherl], 1925). Page references appear in the text.

[6]Rudolf Heinrich Daumann, *Patrouille gegen den Tod. Ein utopischer Roman*, 21.-60. Tausend (Berlin: Schützen Verlag, 1939). Page references appear in the text.

[7]Betina Ewerbeck, *Angela Koldewey. Roman einer jungen Ärztin* (1939; rpt. Ulm: Aegis Verlag, 1950). Page references appear in the text.

[8]Hermann Hoster, *Viele sind berufen. Ein Roman unter Ärzten*, 27.-38. Auflage (Leipzig: Paul List Verlag, 1933). Page references appear in the text.

[9]Theo Malade, *Semmelweis, der Retter der Mütter. Der Roman eines ärztlichen Lebens*, 2. Aufl. (München: J. F. Lehmanns Verlag, 1924).

[10]Hellmuth Unger, *Helfer der Menschheit. Der Lebensroman Robert Kochs* (Leipzig: Verlag der Buchhandlung des Verbandes der Ärzte Deutschlands, 1929). Page references appear in the text.

[11]A. J. Cronin, *Shannon's Way* (Boston: Little, Brown, 1948). Page references appear in the text.

Works Cited

Primary Sources

Anton, Ludwig. *Die japanische Pest.* Leipzig: Ernst Keils Nachfolger (August Scherl), 1925.

Baum, Vicki. *Zwischenfall in Lohwinckel.* Berlin: Verlag Ullstein, 1930.

Cronin, A.J. *Shannon's Way.* Boston: Little, Brown and Co., 1948.

Daumann, Rudolf Heinrich. *Patrouille gegen den Tod. Ein utopischer Roman.* 21.-60. Tausend. Berlin: Schützen Verlag, 1939.

Erlin, W.B. *Die Spur.* Berlin: Die Neue Lese, 1947.

Ewerbeck, Betina. *Angela Koldewey. Roman einer jungen Ärztin.* 1939; rpt. Ulm: Aegis Verlag, 1950.

Fineman, Irving. *Doctor Addams.* New York: Random House, 1939.

Hart, Alan. *The Undaunted.* New York: W. W. Norton and Co., 1936.

Hoster, Hermann. *Viele sind berufen. Ein Roman unter Ärzten.* 27.-38. Auflage. Leipzig: Paul List Verlag, 1933.

Hutchinson, R.C. *The Fire and the Wood: A Love Story.* London, rpt. New York: The Literary Guild of America, 1940.

Koelsch, Adolf. *Narkose. Der Roman vom Kampf gegen den Schmerz.* Zürich: Albert Müller Verlag, 1938.

Lewis, Sinclair. *Arrowsmith.* 1925; rpt. New York: Harcourt, Brace and Co., 1964.

Malade, Theo. *Semmelweis, der Retter der Mütter. Der Roman eines ärztlichen Lebens.* 2. Aufl. München: J. F. Lehmanns Verlag, 1924.

Rabl, Hans. *Die Trennung.* Berlin: Paul Neff Verlag, 1936.

Thompson, Morton. *The Cry and the Covenant.* Garden City, New York: Doubleday, 1949.

Unger, Hellmuth. *Helfer der Menschheit. Der Lebensroman Robert Kochs.* Leipzig: Verlag der Buchhandlung des Verbandes der Ärzte Deutschlands, 1929.

Walker, Mildred. *Medical Meeting.* New York: Harcourt, Brace and Co., 1949.

Weiss, Ernst. *Georg Letham, Arzt und Mörder.* Wien, 1931; rpt. Frankfurt: Suhrkamp, 1982.

Secondary Sources

Benjamin, Philip M. "Books By and About Doctors: A Layman's Check List for 1941." *Bulletin of the Medical Library Association* 30 (1942): 503-512.

Boeschenstein, Hermann. *The German Novel, 1939-1944.* Toronto: U of Toronto P, 1949.

Book Review Digest. All vols., 1907-1950. New York: H. W. Wilson Co.

Carsten, Paul. *Literarisches aus der Medizin, Medizinisches aus der Literatur.* Berlin: Verlag S. Karger, 1931.

Glass, Bentley. "The Scientist in Contemporary Fiction." *The Scientific Monthly* 85.6 (1957): 288-293.

Lingenfelter, Mary Rebecca. *Vocations in Fiction: An Annotated Bibliography.* 2nd ed. Chicago: American Library Association, 1938.

Malmsheimer, Richard Robert. "From Rappaccini to Marcus Welby: The Evolution of an Image." Diss. Univ. of Minnesota 1978.

Norris, Carolyn Brimley. "The Image of the Physician in Modern American Literature." Diss. Univ. of Maryland 1969.

Salmon, Geoffrey. "The Functional Significance of the Physician within the Historical Context of Modern German Literature." Diss. Univ. of Alberta 1978.

Schmitt, Franz Anselm. *Beruf und Arbeit in deutscher Erzählung. Ein literarisches Lexikon.* Stuttgart: Hiersemann Verlag, 1952.

Trautmann, Joanne, and Carol Pollard. *Literature and Medicine: An Annotated Bibliography.* rev. ed. Pittsburgh: U of Pittsburgh P, 1982.

Wachsmuth, Bruno. *Der Arzt in der Dichtung unserer Zeit.* Stuttgart: Ferdinand Enke Verlag, 1939.

West, Mabel C., and Loretta Kreuz. "The Doctor and Nurse in Fiction." *Bulletin of the Medical Library Association* 28 (1940): 198-204.

Wilbanks, Evelyn Rivers. "The Physician in the American Novel, 1870-1955." *Bulletin of Bibliography* 22 (1958): 164-168.

Wittmann, Fritz. *Der Arzt im Spiegelbild der deutschen Literatur seit dem Beginn des Naturalismus.* Berlin: Verlag Dr. Emil Ebering, 1936.

Index

Authors, Historical Medical Researchers, and Literary Works

www.ingramcontent.com/pod-product-compliance
Lightning Source LLC
LaVergne TN
LVHW051641080426
835511LV00016B/2427